MW01601179

Growing a Life Together

Growing a Life Together

FRED M. WOOD

Profile of a Joyful Marriage

BROADMAN PRESS
Nashville, Tennessee

Affectionately dedicated
to
Mitch and Glenda Wood
who are meaning much
to my wife and me
as they are
Growing a Life Together

© Copyright 1975 • Broadman Press
All rights reserved
4283-11 (BRP)

4256-11 (Trade Edition)
ISBN: 0-8054-5611-2 (Trade Edition)

Dewey Decimal Classification: 301.427
Library of Congress Catalog Card Number: 74-81417
Printed in the United States of America

Preface

You want your marriage to be joyful! Of course you do! These nine chapters are designed to help you realize this ambition.

Actually, your "dating years" are paving the way for a successful marriage or one that is a failure. This does not mean merely the time that you spend dating the one whom you marry. Beginning with your first date, you are laying the foundation for the kind of life you will have with the partner of your choice.

Thus, this book begins with a chapter on courtship. It may be you are past that period and feel you should begin reading with chapter 2. On the other hand, you are invited, even if you are already married, to review, perhaps with nostalgia, that glorious period of life that you will never completely forget.

For nearly twenty years I have been the pastor of a church in the busy city where "cross the crowded ways of life." It has been my privilege to counsel with many people concerning problems both before and after marriage.

These years have brought me a deep conviction that a successful marriage depends to a large extent on how closely a couple follows God's will as revealed in the Bible and in Jesus Christ.

God established marriage. The church seeks to guide people into the quality of living that will enable them to succeed in marriage. The church also seeks to help in time of problems and give comfort when sorrow comes.

This book is not a series of sermons. It has come from the overflow of a pastoral ministry which involves personal counseling as well as the delivering of pulpit messages. One month each year for several years, I preached a series of sermons on Love, Courtship, and Marriage. As you would expect, much of the material used in these messages has found its way into this book. I have sought to begin where love begins—with the dating period—and trace the various stages of romance up even until the harvest years. A final chapter is added concerning the place of religion in the home.

These words are set forth in the hope they may help youth and adults alike to find guidance and help in making their marriage an exciting adventure of faith and a creative experience of joy.

Contents

1 *Those Fabulous Dating Years*

What is a date? Excitement! New horizons! The flowering of friendships! The blossoming of personality! New discoveries bring ecstasy and exhilaration to life! The dating years are a time of enthusiasm and eagerness. It is no wonder adults look back upon them with nostalgia and call them "the good old days."

Few remember their second or third date. But most remember the awkward moments of the first one. One now grown lady laughingly recalls how one of her earliest boyfriends was so embarrassed on his first date that on their way home from a high school football game, on a city bus, he handed her a "transfer" and got off at his stop.

Memories that bless and burn!

What about the girl? She must carefully walk a thin line. Her task is to be available without seeming too forward. If a girl flirts, she may run away the "good guys," but if she is too demure or feigns coolness, they may lose interest before they begin. It's enough to scare any girl! She is afraid she lacks "sex appeal." She may feel she is not as pretty as her friends. She is frightened for fear she will be dull. As a result, when she begins to date, she stumbles over her words and half finishes her sentences.

What about the boy? He stands tongue-tied and clumsy. His tongue feels as if it were packed in a big wad of dry cotton. On the other hand, he may go to the opposite extreme if he is inclined to be loud and "talk big" or produce "a fast line" or try to imitate the "successful" boys he has known—often with pathetic results.

Later, however, the fears and inner conflicts will dissolve and each will be his own individual personality. This process may be a long one or short one, depending upon the resourcefulness of the individual.

But Dating Is Not Universal

Our American system of courtship is not, however, a universal phenomenon. In some countries the parents make all the decisions and arrangements for the marriage of their children. Some serious thinkers actually believe this is a better method and more conducive to successful marriage.

One thorough student of the subject says, "The trouble with American marriage is American courtship." According to him, marriage and the rearing of a family is humanity's most important and sacred relationship, and it deserves far more contemplation than we give it. In his opinion, American parents permit and go so far as to encourage their children to choose their lifelong companions in just about the worst of all possible ways.

The "arranged marriage" has a bad connotation in our country. We shed tears for all the poor little girls who are forced into marriage against their will. Yet David and Vera Mace present us with a shocking truth. In *Marriage: East and West* they contend that many of the "victims" of the arranged marriage do not mind it at all. In fact, they point out that when young women from the Far East observe our courtship customs they often feel sorry for the American girls. To them the idea of being forced to go out alone into the open market and seek to secure a husband by scheming and flirting seems undignified and demeaning. One Oriental girl expressed it well. She knew that it was her parents' sacred duty to find her a husband. Thus, she grew up confident that the task would be wisely and capably fulfilled.

Many scholars have pointed out that Oriental literature contains more accounts of happy marriage and more discussion of tender sentiment between husband and wife than Western literature. This leads many students of marriage to contend that perhaps the East has been correct in thinking that the finding and selection of a lifelong companion is too difficult and important a job to trust to immature young people.

There is some truth in these contentions. Dating is not "universal and unmitigated joy." Quite often young people are bored to death even when they are going steady with their "dream lover." When the time comes that they want to break up, they often lack the courage for the painful form of self-assertion it requires. When the break does come, it is a traumatic experience for one or perhaps both. If they have started dating early, this tragedy may be repeated several times during their courting years. We should remember that although today's parents seem to think of the young love affair as a glorious and carefree experience, often there is nothing carefree about it at all.

In all probability, however, our dating system with all its weaknesses is here to stay for a long time. Our society is far different from the older "tightly knit, family centered" societies of other days and other countries.

America is mobile. Young people have no idea where they will live as adults, what jobs they will have, or how much money they will earn. Our system of dating is probably the best and perhaps the only way that young people can shop around and acquire experience enough to end up with the right mate.

Dr. Clifford Kirkpatrick, a sociologist of Indiana University, believes courtship should be regarded as essentially a bargaining process. One goes looking in the open market for the best possible companion to whom his assets entitle him. He believes that many young people set their sights too high and are eternally unsatisfied. Also, however, he thinks a surprising number settle for much less than they could get.

The trial and error method of dating calls for a good, hard, realistic look at the prospective mate. It may, in the long run, produce far better results than the parent-picked companion. At least, it's our American way for the present!

Why Do People Date?

Is there a real purpose in boy-girl get-togethers? Is it merely a matter of a good time and enjoying a few hours of fun and excitement or is the motive deeper? The patterns vary, to be sure, but unquestionably young people are evaluating, deciding, and eliminating during the dating years. Although it can be pleasant recreation and teach many valuable lessons in personal adjustment situations, dating has one basic purpose. It is preparation for and prelude to engagement and marriage. In his book, *Anticipating Your Marriage,* Robert O. Blood, Jr. lists six ways in which dating is preparation for marriage: (1) gaining acquaintances, (2) becoming acquainted with individual personalities, (3) trying out relationships, (4) acquiring skill in human interaction, (5) weaning emotionally from parents, and (6) finding the right person.

Since dating is so vitally related to marriage, some facts are inevitable. First, young people will, or at least should, seek to create the best impression possible on a date. In fact, this is part of the purpose of a date—to put one's best foot forward. Perhaps a girl feels this pressure more than a boy since in our society it is usually the boy who pursues—and proposes. Second, dating can be highly competitive. Boys and girls alike share in this contest for the admiration and affection of the opposite sex. Third, a severe danger follows when dating days are over. Once people are "safely married" they tend to relax and grow careless. Some psychologists believe this is often an unconscious protest against one's companion because of the discipline which one was forced to maintain in order to keep up an image during the courtship period.

The freedom offered by our culture recognizes the importance of dating and even encourages it. In fact, if we are to choose a lifetime partner, we must have training for it in order that the choice may be executed in a mature and responsible manner. Knowledge and understanding are developed through courtship and dating. This is a basic part of the reason for and purpose of dating.

How Do You Get a Date?

To the young person, having a date is of supreme importance. It assures one he is likable, popular, and adequate. It promises that he will be successful in the competitive and threatening adult world of responsibility. The question of how one can be certain to land a date thus becomes extremely important. One prominent editor gives girls some practical suggestions for date getting. She says, "First of all, you must make sure they see you." Other suggestions related to this might be as follows:

(1) Be seen where the boys are, at sports events, rallies, and field practice.
(2) Eat or walk alone. Solid packs of girls can scare off boys while a lone lamb is often appealing.
(3) Be especially courteous to new boys in class.
(4) Smile and greet every one. A friendly girl is more fun to know.
(5) Ask your favorite genius to help you with your homework. (Reward him with freshly baked cookies or brownies.)
(6) Build his ego—ask him to explain a point he made in class or ask his help with a confusing card catalog or library index.
(7) If he's on the defensive in class, smile sympathetically. Never laugh.
(8) Look your best always and you will always be ready if fortune (or a boy) looks your way.

Boys have problems too. Not exactly the same kind as girls, but they are real. Not every boy can get a date every time he wants one in spite of the old cliché, "Girls are like buses—if you miss one, another will be by in a few minutes." Different types have different difficulties.

First, there is the boy who is rather obvious about his reasons for dating a girl. He is interested in exploiting her for sex. Word gets around and girls will avoid him if they have any standards or dignity. No girl, unless she's entirely without self-respect, wants to date a boy who has his mind on this one thing from the start.

Another type of boy with a problem is the one who is shy and awkward. Actually, many girls secretly admire this type and would like to date him, but he must arouse enough self-confidence to ask.

There is also the boy who is so critical of girls he can never quite bring himself to ask a girl for a date very far in advance. After all, a better one may turn up at the last minute and he will be "tied down." These boys usually end up without a date and rationalize by pretending to be "women haters." In reality, they are selfish egotists.

How can a boy get a date? If he will dress neatly, talk politely, be considerate in daily association with everyone, usually he can get a date with almost any girl he wishes unless she is out of circulation because she is going steady. He may not get a date with a girl the first time he asks, but if he will ask again for a specific time, far enough in advance and with courtesy and dignity, he can get a date—usually with his first choice on the campus!

Dating Etiquette

Rhoda L. Lorand in *Love, Sex, and the Teenager* says, "Being out on a date is a host and guest situation. The host has the responsibility of providing a pleasant evening for the guest, and the guest has the obligation of making the occasion as pleasant as possible for the host." If this basic philosophy is kept in mind, dating can be enjoyable and result in a smooth relationship between people. Just as a man has no right to date a girl for "what he can get out of her," neither does she have a right to use him for merely meeting her social, economic, or emotional purposes and needs.

Whose responsibility is it to plan the date? Ideally, it is the boy's, but this does not mean that he should be so overbearing that he refuses any suggestion from the girl. In all probability, the boy, in asking for the first date, should be specific. "Would you like to go with me to the school play next Friday night?" or "Would you like to go to the football game Saturday afternoon?" As the boy and girl come to know each other better, he might ask what she enjoys doing or where she enjoys going. From this he can learn how to suggest a date that she would especially enjoy. It is the boy's responsibility to provide the girl with a happy and wholesome time.

On the other hand, the girl also has obligations. She is to make the boy feel appreciated and secure. If the boy is shy and awkward, she should try to build up his confidence. If he selects a place, she should not start talking about how much she enjoyed being at some other place. Mature girls do not brag about where some other boy took them. (Neither do mature boys boast of dates with other girls.) The girl should make every effort to convey to the boy who is her host for the date that he is pleasing her and that she is enjoying the date. This does not mean that she should be insincere. It does mean, however, that she should honestly try to have a good time and help the boy feel comfortable. In this way he can be happy because he believes she has been pleased with the occasion.

Double-dating

To spend the entire evening with one boy or girl naturally can cause one to have some misgivings. The problem of what to say and even where to go can be a real one. In addition, there is the matter of transportation, financial arrangements, and the general tension accompanying any social occasion. Thus, there are several real advantages to the double date. It is particularly a good arrangement for young people who tend to be shy. One person, with keen insight, said, "Two may be company and three's a crowd, but four is often a party." He suggests that double dates can be "the most beneficial invention for mankind since the wheel, or at least since the electric tooth-brush."

Double dates can, however, turn out to be unmitigated disaster. Almost anyone can remember at least one experience horrifying enough that it sends chills down his back. Something went wrong! For this reason, suggestions are in order concerning proper conduct on a double date. Consider these:

(1) Be willing to accept the group's ideas. Going bowling may not be your idea of an ideal evening, but when the other three "ayes" have it, be gracious.

(2) If you and your steady are double-dating with a boy and girl on their first date, it's your unofficial responsibility to help them have a good time. Save the purely romantic spots for a solo date and plan an evening that won't make the other couple feel uncomfortable.

(3) Even if the other girl is your best friend, reserve female chatter for some other time. Also, refrain from conspic-uously long powder-room huddles.

(4) Don't, though—*please* don't! seize on this double date as your golden opportunity to beau-snatch. Flirting with another girl's date is a cardinal sin, so even if you cherish a secret passion for him, don't make it evident. (This doesn't mean that, some other time, you can't accept an invitation from him. As long as you are not literally run-ning off with your best friend's favorite beau, have no qualms about enlarging your friendship scope this way.)

Undoubtedly, boys need to be warned that they should be sensitive to the emotional feelings and social needs of their dates. It seems, however, that most writers on the subject feel that, on double dates, girls are most likely to commit the faux pas (social blunder) which penalizes them socially and works against future dates. One authority on the social aspects of dating offers some good advice slanted in the direction of girls. He suggests:

First, by all means, remember that a double date is still a *date* and that you should observe all the rules of gracious behavior. Be sure to show your partner the kindness, courtesy, and attention you would if you two were alone. In fact, it's probably a good idea to be even friendlier than you normally would since he may be a little uptight. Making a pass, no matter how subtle, at someone else's date is always poor form, but when four of you are confined to one another's company for an entire evening, it is catastrophic. If you try it and get snubbed in the process, it's only what you deserve.

Second, don't forget that on double dates boys are not as demonstrative as girls. If you can't resist clinging to your boyfriend and holding hands constantly, don't double date since you may embarrass him and everyone else.

Third, the odds, on a double date, are that the girl is a friend of yours. But if you pay too much attention to your mutual interests in the course of conversation, at the expense of the boys, you will end up with more evenings than you would like in each other's company—dateless. The masculine ego is a delicate and sensitive thing. Be very careful not to bruise it.

Fourth, a double date is not a democracy. You shouldn't decide what to do by conducting a referendum. Let the two boys make the arrangements about where and how you will go; don't construct secret alliances or conduct a propaganda campaign. On the other hand, don't be afraid to veto something you don't really want to do. If you have a curfew to make or have already seen that movie, say so. Of course, you should never be obstructive or negative for the sheer joy of it, but if you have a good reason, speak up! Then make the best of it.

Naturally, it helps if all of you share common tastes and preferences. If, however, you are four rugged individualists, each of you should practice the fine art of diplomacy. It can be good training for future adult social responsibilities.

Special Problems and Issues

Financing the date is becoming an increasingly difficult matter for the young man. Because of this the "Dutch date" is becoming popular. Many girls not only do not resent it but actually suggest going Dutch.

A young man in New York states the problem, "I think the time has come for girls to start paying their share of a date. As the system now stands I am forced to subsist on potato chips during the week just so I can afford a Saturday night movie and soda date." It is true that many girls have more money than boys do. At a certain age, girls can actually get jobs easier than boys. Many boys feel that the equal rights girls are demanding carry along with them the obligation for equal responsibilities. If a girl is paying for part of the date, she would not have to feel embarrassed about suggesting an expensive place to go.

Of course, the time has not yet come when the *first* date should be a "Dutch" one. After the couple has been out together several times, however, many feel it is not improper at all for the girl to suggest picking up part (perhaps half) of the tab. One young man from the Northeast suggests: "The girl willing to pay for herself will be the girl with more (fun) dates. Why? Because many boys who have given up dating as a result of the tremendous financial burden would be more than glad to take part in this reasonable arrangement. It makes sense. Think how much more fun it is to hold hands with a boy in a movie than to sit home alone on a Saturday night watching 'The Dating Game.' "

The matter of *how "hard to get" one should play* confuses many girls. One teenager (a girl) has strong feelings about the matter. She maintains, "Dating is not a game and should not be treated as one." She insists that too many times our system of dating has been based on lying and feigned indifference. We have believed that playing "hard to get" is the best way to catch a boy and if we are "too anxious" a boy will lose interest. She contends strongly that the "harmless little lie" is foolish. Pretending to impress the boy by saying you are busy when you are not (merely because the boy has waited late to call you) is not wise. "Fibs grow into big lies," she insists, "that eventually pervade the relationship."

There is a question, of course, about the result in our social relationships if we were 100 percent candid at all times, but the young lady has wisdom in her contention. Honesty is the best policy and insincerity with a boy merely to impress him can lead to serious complications. Good relationships and lasting ones do not come from dishonesty—even early dishonesty that later reforms. To play games and lie concerning our schedule will build walls, and these walls will keep happiness and fulfillment out. Even if you are never caught, it's foolish to treat dating as a game.

The *summer romance* is born in suspension and without roots in real life. When one is away from home and his regular activities, he isolates the present and accents all the happy and lighthearted things about it. When one is in an "away from it all atmosphere," he can live a year in a few short weeks. Affections can ripen quickly—even to an unusual fullness. This type of romance, however, is apt to be like a hothouse flower. It will wither as quickly when one comes back to the distractions of everyday living. The transient fancy can make a delightful summer and a treasured memory if one will treat it this way and let go of the experience when the time is up. The summer romance gives great memories and offers opportunity for hours of later nostalgia but it seldom produces much more. One should avoid taking it too seriously.

Today a new social phenomenon is developing. It is *the black and white date*. Some sections of the country have not yet accepted it but many of the sophisticated schools consider it "no longer avant-garde . . . it's just a little avant-garde." The most popular combination is the black man and white girl.

Parents generally have not accepted interracial dating. A family in Seattle sent their daughter to a psychiatrist when they found out she had dated a Negro while the parents of another girl turned her over to juvenile police as "ungovernable." According to a recent survey, Negro parents are equally adamant in opposing mixed dating. A black man in New York said, "My parents are pretty liberal, but they don't want me to bring home a white girl." In Washington, D.C., a black girl who had been dating both white and black boys said, "My family has told me that really deep down inside, they would rather that I marry a Negro. They say I have a good personality and a good intelligence and they would rather that I pass these things on in the Negro race. I sort of agree with them."

Although one cannot be certain, it is doubtful that interracial dating will be accepted on a large scale in our country for many, many years. Most interracial romances still seem to be mainly exploratory and not very many have actually led to the altar. A Negro girl in New York says, "These relationships really only go so far. There's a point where they break down." The pressures, both from within and without, are usually overwhelming to mixed couples and there is great danger of emotional damage on both sides.

Computer, Blind Dates, and Telephone Tactics

Since 1965 a new craze has been sweeping the nation. At first it was limited to a few college campuses but now it has spread to many parts of the country. A young man named Jeff Parr, a Harvard graduate, put his first punch cards through an IBM computer and gave birth to "Operation Match." Many other similar services have joined the craze and more than three million young people have become involved in the "circulatory-robots turned Cupid" at $2.00 to $5.00 per turn.

The founder of "Operation Match" considers the objectives as modest but crucial. He says, "We just want to take some of the blindness out of blind dates." There have been some ideal situations develop but there have also been many short circuits. For one thing, people will lie about their looks and other qualifications. One young man received a letter from a girl saying he was her dream come true on paper. She sounded good, but when he met her face to face, he recalled later, "I didn't know whether to crowbar her into a cab, or put a saddle on her and ride her home."

There have been some amusing situations. A varsity swimmer at Harvard who was also an amateur astronomer advertised that he was looking for someone who would time his laps in the pool and be willing to wake up at 3 A.M. to watch comets with him. The computer digested the information and squeezed out an auburn-haired Radcliffe girl who was fed up with pseudointellectuals. She wanted someone who enjoyed sports. They developed into steadies.

This leads to a discussion of *blind dates* which are very closely related to the computer program except that usually the person who chooses the blind date does so with less scientific data. Usually, it is just the person's own idea of who would be good for someone or else a convenient friend who needs a date supplies the partner.

A survey on blind dates revealed a number of strong comments—both ways. A girl in Maryland said, "A blind date? Not for me—so long as I have good sight in both eyes." A girl in Illinois, however, says, "Most girls don't like blind dates but I think they are all right if arranged by friends you know wouldn't fix you up with some 'goof.' In fact, I had one blind date that worked out so well he's now my fiance." A girl in Nebraska warns, "If you are not sure what you are walking into, you'd better stay put." A boy in Maine says, "I don't see any need for blind-dating. If a boy or girl wants to go on a date, he or she should get to know the other person first." But a boy in the state of Washington said, "From experience I have found that blind dates are really a lot of fun. I always look forward to them."

If one decides to accept a blind date, he should remember that he is obligated to be a lady or a gentleman with kindness and courtesy throughout the evening even if he draws a blank.

The modern Romeo has an indispensable courting device which serves as an electronic balcony. It is the *telephone*. It's great for the girl also. She doesn't even have to put on lipstick or comb her hair to score points. One surveyor reminds us that more than a fourth of most boy-girl relationships take place on the telephone.

A girl should be wise in her telephone tactics. At the start, the feminine role is largely that of listener. Since she is usually the one who is being called, she should never underestimate the creative art of listening. The girl should realize that most boys had rather face a charging rhinoceros than call a girl they admire. Boys are usually terrified lest they be turned down. A wise girl can help pull a boy through by drawing him out, laughing at his jokes and encouraging him to talk about things that interest him. For a girl to say "that's interesting" to a boy or "you're too much" can raise his ego as much as a dozen red roses can raise hers.

The telephone date may be divided into several phases. First, there is the "breaking the ice." Second, the couple comes to the "how are you's." This is usually the most monotonous part of the conversation. A smart person will not spend too much time on it. Third, there is "the grand dialogue" which is the "heavenly stuff of which talkathons are made." This is followed by the "popping the question." After the date is made, there is a smart way of "tuning out" and leaving your phone partner with joyful anticipation of the time when you will see each other face to face.

Dating and Harmful Substances

Not too many years ago (back in the "good old days"), parents used to worry about whether their teenagers were smoking or drinking. Today, however, they are also worrying about something else dreadfully dangerous—drugs. Because of the extreme seriousness of drugs, many parents have forgotten that alcohol and tobacco can have harmful effects, too.

Today, the college, high school, and even junior high school campuses are being flooded with narcotics ranging from the depressants ("goof balls") and stimulants ("pep pills") through marijuana ("pot," "grass") to the hallucinogens (including STP and LSD) that send young minds spinning off in "wild and unpredictable journeys through stunningly beautiful visions or terrifying nightmares."

Books have been devoted to this problem and young people would do well to familiarize themselves with the facts. The question here is the relationship of dating a boy or girl who is a user of drugs, or of alcohol, for that matter. Again, it is difficult to know what figures are accurate. Estimates vary. Some of the more sophisticated periodicals print surveys showing that an almost unbelievable number of students are experimenting with drugs in one form or another. Publications by people in the educational field are more conservative and tend to play down the number, suggesting it is greatly exaggerated in contemporary periodicals.

Because of the drug epidemic, however, many people have overlooked the increasing popularity of alcoholic beverages among young people. Beer, ale, and the sweet-tasting "pop" wines with relatively high alcohol content are coming into vogue among many youth. They excuse themselves with the drinking of alcohol, even 86 or 100 proof, by alibiing, "It's not as bad as drugs." Many experts believe that the long-range use of alcohol can be almost as bad. Day by day alcoholic beverages are also gaining a foothold among youth because many parents and officials feel alcohol (which is really a drug) "is not as bad as drugs."

The question of whether one should date a person who is experimenting with drugs is somewhat different from the old question of whether to date a person who smoked or even drank moderately. The problems in the use of the more severe drugs are more far-reaching. This is not the place, of course, for a technical analysis of the effects of drugs upon the body and mind. Nevertheless, some common-sense thinking is in order.

A young man or woman who drinks alcohol can sober up and be "normal" on a date. The fact that he was drinking last week does not mean, necessarily, that he is affected on the night of the date. This is not true, however, with the strongest drugs. We are still in the investigative period concerning the effects of the various types. Some have delayed effects. This means that a person might perform some "way out" act on a date because of his previous use of drugs, for instance LSD. Thus, it's just plain good sense to be cautious about dating those who are experimenting with drugs in any way. Care should also be applied to the matter of dating those who use alcoholic beverages.

Now I'm not "big brother" trying to control your life. You'll have to make the decisions and then live with them. Be careful.

What about the emotional life of those who are either "hooked" on a harmful substance or at least experimenting with one? Again, it is difficult to generalize but some of the reasons given by students for using them are: bravado, boredom, curiosity, or escapism. Some have said they do so because they don't want to be called "chicken." A New York University survey concluded that adolescents who used drugs suffered from deep-rooted personality disorders, were cynical about life, and had a general feeling of futility. A wise young person will be extra cautious about becoming involved with a person who fits this category of behavior.

Affection on a Date

Everyone wants to be accepted and appreciated! The need to be reassured periodically that we are attractive and desirable is normal. One who denies this is not honest with himself. As we grow older, we seek affection from those our age of the opposite sex. The dating period is an excellent time to show and receive the right kind and proper amount of affection.

What is the "right kind" and "proper amount"? In our American way of life we have assumed affection is best shown first by holding hands and then by kissing. Other stages develop in the process of further courtship. A former high-ranking staff member for the American Medical Association gives an excellent statement for those in the early years of dating: "Obviously, a boy and girl who are very fond of each other may wish to walk hand in hand or . . . enjoy holding hands in the movies, or sitting close together on hayrides. They may greet each other or say goodnight with a kiss. But if they are wise, they will let it go at that."

Most of us feel inadequate to attempt any further statement of guidelines. We prefer to think common sense should take over in the crisis situations. A suggestion or two, however, might be in order. Why, for instance, do people need physical expressions of affection? To be sure, at specific ages in bodily growth we feel the need for physical contact, but is there not sometimes more involved? What type of boy feels compelled to exploit a girl physically? Isn't it the one who doubts himself and his ability? The young man who is completely secure does not need to bolster his deflated ego by mauling every little girl he dates and demanding that she be pliable and yield to his every whim.

The same is true of the girl. Only the love-starved young lady actually wants excessive displays of physical affection. There is, of course, the socially insecure girl who will allow a boy to exploit her against her real wishes because she feels it is "future date insurance." If a girl has more concern about her social status than she has self-respect for her body and character, she will probably allow herself to be caressed and fondled at will—and perhaps more. This is a decision she must make. It is in the realm of value judgment. She should remember, however, that buying dates by handing out such favors will not buy the best dates, and the time will come when this kind of currency is "deflated" on the dating market.

Another, and far more important, fact both boys and girls need to remember is that there are other ways of showing affection besides physical expressions. Kindness, courtesy, and thoughtfulness show that one cares for another. Planning activities together which build respect for each other's personality—sharing of mutual interests and hobbies—a surprise gift now and then—these are true expressions of affection. Dating does not have to begin with or degenerate to a mere physical relationship. By mental creativity, dates can be wholesome, enjoyable, and even character building. These kinds are really much more fun and leave far happier memories behind.

What About Going Steady?

Most adults fail to realize "going steady" has changed in meaning since their courting days. It is no longer "engaged to be engaged." Unless one is knowledgeable in this area, he has a serious communication gap with the dating generation.

Today, "going steady" among the high school or college students means that at this stage in one's social life, two people have an understanding they date only each other. It may change later, but *now* the matter is already settled as to whom one's date is at the current social functions. One "not too worried" adult said, "It's a habit, going steady; it's a convenience, making sure they have a partner."

Are there advantages in this type of arrangement? As one teenager said, "You'd better believe it!" It certainly relieves pressure. A girl does not have to wonder whether she will have a date for Friday night. She already has one! She can relax and devote her time to study without anxiety. Let's be fair. This has its advantages. The boy, likewise, finds it convenient. He is relieved of the responsibility for making a decision. Since he has committed himself, he is not continually seeking new fields to conquer. At least, he shouldn't be!

Is there a basic "in depth" psychology behind "going steady"? Frankly, in certain social sets, it's the only way to rate. If you are going to get invitations, you must have "a steady." But there is more to it than that! Having a steady date represents personal fulfillment. It shows others and oneself that "I can do it." It becomes an achievement symbol!

After many years of experience in his field, one mature counselor summarizes articulately the advantages, "There are, of course, arguments in favor of it. It gives a girl a sense of security against being a wallflower, and assures a boy of a date for important events. The boy and girl who go steady get to know each other very well, may enjoy each other's company all the more for that reason. There is a definite satisfaction in knowing that a certain individual is always ready to participate in activities as your partner. Going steady helps to build up your self-respect."

Going Steady Presents Problems

Now, let's look at the other side. Going steady narrows the field. Everyone wants to choose the best possible person for a life partner. This is the major purpose of dating. Going steady could cause one to sell himself short of exploring the field.

Steady dating tends to discourage personality development. Different people bring out different undeveloped traits within us. Unless we discover these truths before marriage, we may learn them suddenly and shockingly after marriage. By dating many different people, we can get a true index into our own character and personality.

One of our modern marriage counselors speaks of what every man needs to have in courtship in order to assure a well rounded preparation for marriage: "Specifically a fellow should have had the emotional experience of being with a girl who made him feel tenderly protective, with another whose hand he could clasp with a feeling of hearty comradeship, with another whose feminine appeal sent his blood to his face and his heart to his throat, with another who made him as comfortable and easy as a sister, and perhaps with still another who brought forth a pleasant combination of all these feelings in a satisfying mixture." Girls likewise need to know the various types of boys. Going steady prevents this experience.

The progressive intimacy in personal relationships cannot be ignored. There develops a feeling of "belonging to each other." Special privileges come to be expected. There is a tendency to explore new territory on each date. What brought a thrill last week is "old hat" next week. You run out of something to talk about and you lapse into physical expressions of affection. As one columnist said, "Quicker than a penguin sliding down an icicle—that's how quickly a petting session can turn into a jam session and you're the one in the jam!"

An outstanding writer in the field of marital relationships has a special word for girls who are going steady. She doesn't warn them about the usual things—pregnancy and venereal disease—but rather speaks with cool common sense about dignity and self-respect. She says: "Remember it's always the girl who suffers most in 'giving in.' Chances are she hasn't really enjoyed it—it will be years before the pure happiness of sexual fulfillment will be hers; her body was made that way. She may not become pregnant. She may not face an abortion. Her parents may not have caught her. She may not get venereal disease. But what has she gained? Not the boy's respect. Not love, for the male's sex urge is not a thing of love. Not the security of a steady date, for he may turn quickly away from an 'easy make.' She may well wonder 'Was it worth it?'—what has the sexual act done for her? Sex is a lifelong emotional thing, not a teenage crisis. Sexual love is something too valuable to be spoiled by misuse. Say 'No,' little girl. You will not be sorry." These words are relevant—extremely relevant—for many couples who have become steadies.

There is another problem. How do you get out? There are those who have become tired but hate to hurt each other by suggesting a separation. In a few cases they never did feel deeply but rather drifted into the relationship accidentally and suddenly discovered they were each tied to the other. Perhaps people assumed they were going steady and identified them with each other until they took the path of least resistance and became steadies.

There are three practices in general use today. The *love-'em and leave-'em* variety is characteristic of one method. This is quick, easy, and effective. It was there yesterday. It isn't today. One or the other just doesn't respond any more. He doesn't call her or drop around or she isn't in when he calls. This is effective but usually hurts are inflicted. The one jilted has hurt feelings and the one who ran away feels remorse of conscience. There can be *agonizing discussions* about "how washed up we are." This kind of break drags on uncomfortably. An old saying, "If you have to cut off the puppy's tail, do it in one blow" might be helpful here but it's still painful. The *easing off type of break* blends an acceptance of the situation with some understanding on the part of each. Whatever method is used, one should seek to employ the kindest and yet the most effective skills of which he is capable.

It Can Be Fun

Although dating has been defined as "education in the discovery of emotions and their control," it still can be fun! The gestures of affection during this period can enrich one's life if they are tied in with the discovery of common interests and goals. Dating can train young people in the "art of democratic give and take." To conclude this chapter, some rules for personality development are suggested that can make you a more fulfilled person and a more interesting date. They will also help you to have fun during the fabulous dating years:

1. Be yourself. Set your own standards and ideals—then stick with them.

2. Accept yourself for what you are. You can have heroes and imitate people you admire, but you become an adult only when you accept yourself and then endeavor to improve that

self by seeking broader horizons.

3. Accept others as they are. Don't pick on their weaknesses and, above all, never humiliate them. Recognize their good points and appreciate them.

4. Be friendly. Remember that glum and sour people live lonely lives.

5. Be an interesting person. Have many interests outside yourself. Remember that others are not really concerned with your feelings, hurts, worries, and petty weaknesses. You will not be interested either if you live new hobbies, cultivate your abilities, and always be looking for new experiences and friends.

Your dating years should and can be fabulous!

2 *Looking Forward to Settling Down*

A minister was counseling a young lady concerning the problems of her love life, or lack of it. He said, "The Lord has one woman for every man and one man for every woman. That's God's plan and you can't improve on it." She replied, "I don't want to improve on it. I just want to *get in on it!*" Most normal people want to get married. There comes a time when we're ready to quit "playing the field" and settle down to a life's companion.

Are You Ready?

In most activities, timing is of superlative importance. Many marriage counselors say it is more important to know *when* to get married than to know *whom* to marry. If there is a "time for all things," surely there is a time to marry and a time to refrain from marrying.

Are you ready, emotionally? Marriage requires many qualities, and one of the chief of these is emotional maturity. None of us has ever completely arrived, but there must be an element of maturity before one should even consider taking this important step.

No relationship is so intimate as marriage. Yet, it involves two people who have had no previous experience of knowing the other except in a superficial way. There will be new demands, personality changes, and financial adjustments. There will be many decisions to make.

31

One should face some questions about himself honestly. Am I capable of sharing my possessions with another? Can I receive criticism without becoming resentful and angry? Do I have personal habits which can easily be offensive to my proposed companion? Can I really love someone else as much as I love myself? Have I honestly forsaken all desire to love another person of the opposite sex as I love the one whom I plan to marry? If you ask, "Is it possible to love two people at the same time?" there is a strong possibility you are not yet ready for marriage. You are enjoying one of life's growing periods, but mature love has not yet come to you.

Are you ready, agewise? How old should one be before marrying? This depends, of course, on a number of factors. A difference in social background, self-development, and educational level all play their part. One person may be ready for marriage at twenty while another may not be ready at thirty. Every serious study, however, has pointed up the wisdom of refraining from a teenage marriage. According to one survey, marriages in the 15-19 age bracket are three-and-one-half times more likely to fail than those in the 25-29 age bracket. In general, studies advocate a man being the minimum of 22 and a girl at least 19 to 21. A few years older is probably a bit more desirable for the percentages to favor a permanent relationship.

Are you ready, economically? A young man, recently married, wrote to his brother, "I've found that two can live as cheap as one, but *only half as long.*" In addition to the regular problems of marriage, there are special problems for those who marry before they are able to command good salaries. Since teenage newlyweds lack advanced education, they usually have a low earning power even if both work. Many times parents are willing to help. This, however, may cause the problem of emotional involvement by the parents in the new marriage. Young newlyweds are seldom able to obtain sufficient credit for the setting up of a household. Once they get it, they tend to "go overboard." Heavy installments are dangerous for young people with limited earning power. Many teenagers have had material possessions bordering upon luxury at home such as washers, air conditioning, and cars. Too often, they expect that marriage will automatically bring these to them immediately. The result is they buy impulsively and become frustrated if they have to wait. Having limited savings, if any, they are plunged into a financial crisis when faced with job loss, unexpected pregnancy, illness, or an accident.

Facts to Face

There is a great deal of difference in the way two people look to each other *before* marriage and *after*. A boy is usually more interested during courting days in the girl's feminine charm than whether she would be a comfort to him or criticize him severely if he lost his job. The girl, too many times, is more concerned with his outward displays of masculinity than in whether he is mature enough to accept responsibility for a family. One seminary professor expressed it this way: "There sets in shortly after marriage what is known as a process of reevaluation." A student, recently married, said, "Boy, that's the understatement of the year." As one cynic put it:

> If he's sympathetic and his words are tender
> After she's just creased a fender
> If he is calm and his hands don't shake
> After she's cremated a sirloin steak;
> If he's chivalrous as King Arthur's gallants
> When her checkbook doesn't balance
> There's one thing you can safely bet
> He and she aren't married yet.

Why do people choose each other? Much has been said about love springing from "a meshing of basic needs." There is, of course, much truth in this concept. We all want people to act in a certain way toward us. When a person finds someone who helps him to function in accord with his underlying motivations, love develops. For instance, if a man likes to dominate, he will be inclined to seek a submissive woman. This type of woman will probably be attracted to a dominating man. Often, the selection of a mate with complementary needs is not a conscious, deliberate procedure. One may not be aware of his own needs, let alone those of a prospective spouse. If you ask him what he sees in her, he will cite some ill-defined attribute such as, "She's kind and gentle." She says she finds him irresistible because he's "so vibrant and happy." A probing psychiatrist may discover that the man really wants to be mothered. He subconsciously perceives a mothering disposition in the woman's solicitous attitude. She, on the other hand, may be one who sees in his high spirits a little boy who has to be taken care of. Perhaps similar backgrounds and similar ideas bring couples together. The complementary needs, however, are those that lead the acquaintance toward a permanent union.

Many studies have been made concerning factors that work for permanent marriages. It has been found that certain conditions indicate greater proneness to divorce. Facts such as these should be faced frankly by the one who is seriously considering marriage. There is general agreement among sociologists that the following are major contributors to divorce:

(1) Urban background
(2) Marriage at 15-19 (the teenage divorce rate is about three times the general rate)
(3) Short acquaintance before marriage
(4) Parents had unhappy marriages
(5) Nonattendance at church
(6) Mixed faith
(7) Disapproval of marriage by relatives and friends
(8) Dissimilarity in social and economic status
(9) Differing ideas between husband and wife

Another fact which should be faced is that of the difference between men and women. Byron says,

> Man's love is of man's life a thing apart;
> 'Tis woman's whole existence.

There is quite a contrast between the analytical, practical outlook of the male and the woman's more introspective and intuitive approach to things. If men were more like women, we might not have pyramids, bridges, and supersonic transports. These require systematic intelligence to design and a ruthless single-mindedness to execute. On the other hand, if men were more like women, there would be less blunders in the delicate area of human relations.

As we look forward to "settling down," we need to remember that a man is not a woman and a woman is not a man. This difference continues on through every stage of marriage. In even the little adjustments around the house we see it. One woman jokingly complained about her husband:

> In marital altercations
> I've learned to compromise
> On mornings we can sleep
> Why can't we synchronize?
> When I have no breakfast to fix
> He will wake and rise at six.

Differences need not trouble us, however, if we remember that God made these differences for a purpose. To be a man or woman means to differ but each complements the other. The difference involved is not only biological but also extends to the whole person, contributing to each partner the meaning of fulfillment. Not only do we need to *recognize* the differences, but we need to *emphasize* the fact that each was made for the other. By means of the particular and unique gifts possessed, each is able to serve the other.

What Do You Want?

Many surveys have been made on college campuses, in church groups, and elsewhere to determine what type of girl boys want to marry and vice versa. What characteristics are most appealing? Most of us know the traits that rate highest—neatness, natural-

ness, sense of humor, friendliness, and unselfishness. The fallacy
is that these are opinions of single people who do not yet know
what they really want. They may think they do, and often their
opinions are good but they do not speak from personal experience. Can they really know what they want?

It seems another kind of survey is in order. What do married
people think, ten years or more later, are the most important
elements in a husband or wife? One concept cherished by most
Americans is that of a romantic and companionable marriage—
Mary and John take each other for the sheer pleasure of living
together. This covenant is sealed with a kiss . . . the "happy
portent of lifelong closeness."

How realistic is this concept? Two studies were made recently
in the sociology department of a large university. The first was
with 299 young housewives in the suburbs representing a wide
social and economic range. The second study involved 323 urban
housewives of various racial and religious groupings. The subur-
ban women were in their early thirties and had been married
an average of ten years. The city women were older. Both groups
were each given two-hour interviews. The first question asked
was, "What are the roles of a woman in order of importance
in a marriage?" It is interesting that only 28 percent of the young
wives (married on an average of ten years) thought that "wife"
was the most important role. The far greater majority in both
groups ranked "mother" as the most important role. The real
core of the research was revealed in the answers to another
question, "What are the roles (in order of importance) of the
man in the family?" Sixty-three percent of the young women
and 64 percent of the older women listed "breadwinner" (or
"provider") in first place. Sixty-five percent put "father" second.
The role of "husband" was a weak third. Only 13 percent of
the young women and 16 percent of the older women put
"husband" as the most important role.

Another conclusion reached from this survey was that wives
cared far more about what their husbands *did* than about what

they *were* as persons. The writer is making no attempt at "value judgment" on this point but only emphasizing its pragmatic significance for those who are thinking of "settling down" to a life's companion.

What should marriage be and how can we make it what it ought to be? In an article entitled "Is It Immature Loving?" Frank Wessling says, "Marriage is a promise to make two into one. Two people as different as they can be—man and woman—promise to make an attempt to immerse their separate prior selves into a new self, a synthesis forged in the time-fires of struggle, joy, conflict, pain, ecstasy, fear—all the jolting glory of human life well lived." This cannot be done with a mere physical sexual relationship. Wessling spoke of his own personal marital experience by saying that he and his wife found their moments of intimacy and self-giving did not need to be confined to the bedroom. He said, "My wife and I think there is joy in filling the envelope with all the small, daily love-making we can."

Before one decides to marry, he should be sure he has decided what he wants in a marriage and in a companion. Decide whether you are in love with a person or *in love with love.* Too often, falling in love has about the same relation to love as the idea for a story has to do with the ordeal of its writing. Love is not an end in itself but the vision that enables us to embark upon and, if it is strong enough and we are strong enough, to endure the ordeal of loving.

Now and Then

There is a complication about the maturing of boys and girls which should be remembered in choosing a companion. If a boy nineteen years old marries a girl of the same age, she will likely become a woman quite a bit before he will become a man. The girl of nineteen may find the boy's immaturity and self absorption actually appealing since it mirrors her own. She will be a lot less pleased, however, when she grows up at twenty-two or twenty-three, and the boy does not mature so rapidly.

Of course, the hazard may be just the opposite. The boy may grow up (a few years later) and find that the girl he picked has not matured. Why? Because, as a boy, he chose a girl who did not offer too much competition in the brain department, who was pretty in a conventional and superficial sort of way, and whose immaturity and shallowness matched his own. Later, the boy grows up but the girl doesn't. He wants a woman of developed character. The girl who appealed to him as a boy seems, at twenty-five, unendurably thin, boring, empty, and even revolting. Many very pretty girls become ordinary women. Many of the girls, however, who are very plain now are going to be the beauties in a few years. When they have found their grip on life, generosity, warmth, and kindliness will shine in their faces. They will then be superlatively attractive. It may well be that the powerful feelings of desire that now torment a young man have nothing more behind them than average health, regular use of a good shampoo, a clear skin, and the absence of any challenging qualities. Boys, remember the fact that a young girl with only physical beauty is not an adequate foundation for a lifetime's happiness.

Don't Be Afraid

In spite of all the problems involved, however, marriage is a marvelous way of life. A man is only half a man until he is married. Although it is an old cliche, it is true—behind every successful and happy man is a good woman. Someone once asked a prominent celebrity whether she would settle for less than the ideal man. She replied, "Ask yourself this: If you did find an ideal man, would he marry you?" The truth is that after all the studies have been made and all safeguards taken, we can never be sure of marrying the right person. She also said, with tongue in cheek, "Marrying a man is like having your hair cut short. You won't know whether or not it suits you until it's too late to change your mind."

These last words are not an attempt to cancel or minimize the previous discussions of this chapter. It is simply to say that even as we cannot refuse to bring children into the world because the days are dangerous, neither can we refuse to marry because the risks are great. Let us face it frankly. Few people settle down to accepting the responsibilities of life until they are in their own home with their own obligations and duties confronting them. There will be problems, many of them, but there are compensations in the endless vista of love. There is much you do not know but remember that the beauty of human relations is that we are not required to have total knowledge all at once.

It takes courage to decide you are ready to settle down. A real marriage is not a refuge for two fearful people. It is a point of embarkation for two brave souls of faith. Too many young lovers come to marriage not as pioneers looking foward to building a new life, but as refugees seeking to escape the old. Be sure you are not expecting marriage to eliminate your unpleasant problems—family discipline, school work, restraint, loneliness, routine or boredom with your situation, place, job, or self. Marriage is not a "never-never land of problems."

Be honest with yourself and your motivation. Do not seek to escape into the "pseudo-security" of a too early marriage. If, however, you have found one with whom you are ready to share your life, if you two have faced the issues fairly, if you have analyzed the financial picture, if you are ready—then go to it! Ask God to help you. Remember that "Unless the Eternal builds the house (or home), they labor in vain who build it."

3 *So You're Engaged!*

A young lady was showing her girl friends her new engagement ring. She said, "There's one thing for sure. I didn't accept the first time Jim proposed." One of her friends retorted, "You bet you didn't, honey. You weren't there." Another girl was having trouble getting the other girls to notice her engagement ring. She finally said, "It surely is warm in here. I think I'll take off my ring."

Usually we think of the engagement period as being important mostly to the woman. The cynical male would say that engagement is a necessary evil in order that a girl may have her picture in the paper and have a number of parties and showers. Other, more practical men, however, see the advantage of such showers because of the gifts involved. They'll sure come in handy!

Is Engagement Necessary?

Of all the means that lie within the power of counselors and sociologists to influence marriages in the direction of success and away from failure, adequate preparation *before* is probably the one likely, at present, to prove most effective. For this reason, and others, your engagement is far more important than you think. To the superficial thinker, engagement appears to be a useless and tantalizing waiting period before marriage. If we're really in love, why wait?

There are real values in a period of engagement. The time spent in such a period brings many dividends later on. Engagement has been called "a necessary bridge between the irresponsibility of youth . . . and the married responsibility of adults." This period is quite different from the courtship. It is a time of planning life together. Other people are forgotten. The two think only of each other and their future. The engagement is a time of testing, of preparation, of growing understanding and intimacy. During this period personalities are adjusted to each other. The little rough edges that often irritate each other and cause tension are polished and refined.

Annoying habits are discussed more freely than during the courtship period. In *Being Married* by Evelyn M. Duvall and Reuben Hill, seven advantages of the engagement period are suggested.

> (1) The engagement saves a man from being dazzled by the supposed glamor of his fiancee, since it gives him opportunities to see her in everyday clothes over a period of time.
> (2) The engagement enables both to become much better acquainted with the other's family and to become accepted by them.
> (3) The engagement provides the opportunity to create an amorous monopoly in which "old flames" and rivals are eliminated as love objects.
> (4) The engagement provides insight into the relative responsiveness of the other.
> (5) The engagement gives full opportunity to discuss children, child discipline, wife working, handling of money, extra-marital friendships and other vital issues which often don't seem appropriate in the dating and courtship stages.
> (6) The engagement provides time to arrange financial affairs and to gradually get ready for the economic burden of marriage.
> (7) The engagement gives both participants a chance occasionally to slip into the roles of husband and wife to learn some of the ropes while still in the engagement period.[1]

It is true, of course, that an engagement period may not be *absolutely essential* to a marriage. There have been many successful and happy marriages without such a period. Consecrated common sense, however, will recognize the wisdom of having a period between the time of decision to marry and the actual time of the wedding. In fact, an outstanding feminine personality recently made an interesting observation about the subject. She said, "One of the nicest things about marriage happens before it even starts—courtship. It should last awhile. These days of engagements are growing shorter and so, alas, are many of the marriages that follow." Actually, the months of engagement are eye-openers. A girl is destined to be amazed at what she will learn about a man only *after* she gets the ring. That's because she starts sizing him up for the first time, not as a date, but as a potential husband. She now begins to examine the more serious side of him—whether he can finance a marriage, how he feels about children, what he might be like to live with on a day-to-day instead of a Saturday-night-to-Saturday-night basis. If a girl doesn't find out these answers, she takes the short odds in matrimony. She's likely to come running back to mother weeping because her "dream boat" has turned out to be a "tramp steamer."

Activities During Engagement

What should be the program during engagement? There are some definite things to *do*. Suppose you have just become engaged and are ecstatically happy. What will you want to do first? That's easy to answer! You will want to tell the world how happy you are! Remember, however, that the first people you should tell, unless there is some unusual reason, are the parents of both of you. There may be exceptions to this rule, but not often. Even if you are planning to marry someone of whom your parents disapprove, you should tell them. They deserve to know it before anyone else. They have reared you and made sacrifices for you. It is their right to be included from the start in your happiness. From the practical standpoint, if you expect opposition from them, it may cushion the blow to them and help smooth the pathway if they hear the news from you and not from someone else first. Tell your parents. You will be glad you did.

Next, usually comes the engagement ring. Few men have one in their pocket when they propose. Is an engagement ring an absolute necessity? Of course not! But on the other hand it makes good sense to place a high value on its importance. An engagement ring is a symbol and a pledge. The truth is, very few girls, if they are honest with themselves, dislike the idea of receiving one. But if your fiancé's means are slender, perhaps you would prefer instead that he use the money toward your new life together. Someday he can buy you the sort of ring he wants you to possess for life. In any event, if you are truly in love, you will prefer the smallest diamond, or any other stone—your birthstone, for instance—to having him spend more than he can for a more impressive ring.

A practical suggestion to the man is as follows: Go to the jeweler and price the rings. Tell him about how much you can afford. Choose several within this range. Bring your fiancée to the jeweler and let her choose from this selection. If none of these please her exactly, the jeweler will know to show her others in your price range. If she's too stubborn and hard to please, you might want to rethink this matter of marriage immediately! This may be the pattern of her actions in all things!

Not necessarily third, but somewhere along the line, premarital counseling is in order. Many ministers insist on a schedule of conferences with those for whom they perform the ceremony. This is excellent. Some ministers are especially prepared for this type of counseling because of special study which they have done. Even those ministers who do not insist on one or more conferences should be glad to do so upon request. In fact, if the minister whom you have chosen refuses to counsel with you before marriage, it is doubtful whether he is the kind of person you would want to perform your ceremony.

The matter of premarital counseling cannot be overemphasized. There are many fine service organizations which specialize in this type of work. One such organization has a notable success record. It has been in existence more than twenty years and only a very small number of those couples which have used its premarital counseling service have ended in divorce. This is uniquely significant, since this particular organization is located in a section of the country where divorce rates are among the highest.

Surely no one will debate the fact that much disappointment and suffering can be spared a young couple if they can be told before they marry that they are unsuited for each other because of radical differences in character, temperament, culture, and religious outlook. Before the lifelong vows are pronounced is the time when counsel and guidance are most urgently needed and will do the most good. If you are afraid to look at each other realistically in a counseling session, you are too immature for marriage.

One marriage counselor says that a third of our divorces could be prevented if a wise counselor talked the situation over with young people before the wedding. Not all weddings should be called off because of differences in the couple. We are all different. A counseling period can help a couple to understand each other and facilitate the process of adjustment in married life. Some type of premarital counseling is most essential. Don't ignore this during the engagement period.

Choosing the date of the wedding, where it will be held, and how large or small it will be are matters of personal preference. These are settled during the engagement period. The bride will, of course, have the final choice of the exact date, although the general period of time will be a matter of mutual agreement. Opinions vary concerning how much money should be spent on a wedding. There are some who believe it makes good sense to spend only a nominal amount on the wedding and enter marriage in better financial condition. Some parents who can afford to give their daughter a large wedding prefer to give a small wedding and give the bride and groom a lovely honeymoon for a wedding present. Some girls, however, would rather have a beautiful wedding to which they can look back with happy memories.

Do not overlook the importance of the honeymoon. Some marriages never get over the scars of an unhappy honeymoon. The purpose of this time is to get the "shared life" begun under the best possible circumstances. Every newly married couple ought to have some time together, apart from family and friends, and apart from the normal routine of work and social life, so that they can begin, without outside interference, their life together. They should go to a place where other people will pay little attention to them, where there are no schedules to meet, and no unusually difficult circumstances. More will be said about this later, but the engagement period is the time to plan the honeymoon.

Another important activity is the matter of a complete physical examination. Most states require some kind of superficial certification, but it usually concerns a blood test for communicable disease or perhaps a guarantee against feeblemindedness. To have more than these guarantees is a mark of great wisdom. A complete and frank discussion of each person's health with the other is only fair to both parties. If one enters marriage with some kind of health problem, the other is apt to resent it if he is not told beforehand. Especially will this be true if it will require financial outlay throughout the years. Perhaps you have heard of the newly married girl who had to have her tonsils removed. The doctor told the couple that she should have had it done when she was a small child. The groom sent the bill to his father-in-law! Also, the physician can give instruction or advice concerning problems related to the sexual aspect of married life. Few people have a completely thorough physical check-up before marriage, but it should be done.

Settling Some Problems

In addition to activities, there are attitudes to form as a couple looks forward to a lifetime together. Have you ever stopped to think that one of the biggest responsibilities in life choice-wise must be made during the earliest years of one's life? While we are still young and limited in the experience of living, we must choose the person with whom we will share life in the most intimate of all human relations for perhaps fifty years.

Differences may attract temporarily, but it will take agreement in a basic philosophy of life to produce a marriage which grows in compatability through the years. We should utilize every resource available to help us in synthesizing our attitudes toward life in order that we may have a happy home. During the engagement period you think together about the practical, everyday matters of living.

You should discuss freely the matter of your economic life. How much money does he make? Will it be necessary for her to continue working? Will you have separate bank accounts? Will either have to support or help a parent or some other relative? How much furniture do you expect to buy immediately? Do you have two cars now? Will you continue to have two? Which one will you sell? Which person will drive the car to work if both continue employment? If the bride becomes pregnant sooner than expected, can you live on one salary? Do you expect to receive help from either set of parents? Complete frankness is necessary in order that you will enter marriage with no misunderstandings.

What about a family? Are you agreed as to whether you want children or not? Are you agreed, in the main, about when you want them? To discuss birth-control methods during engagement is not improper and is even wise. The visit to the doctor for a physical check-up can include a frank discussion about birth-control methods. If one of the two is a Catholic, an honest and realistic approach must be made to the Roman Catholic Church's position on birth control.

The matter of church membership and plans for attendance cannot be ignored. Unless a couple is completely without spiritual inclinations (if they are, they had better stop and think seriously as to whether they are ready for such an important step as marriage), they will want to decide about worship together. Every poll taken shows that mixed marriages, religiously speaking, have greater odds against their permanency. If the two can agree on the same church, without sacrificing personal convictions, it is far better to be together in one church and rear the children in that church. One should examine his motives and be completely honest in this realm. If one has strong convictions in a certain direction, he should be very careful in contending for his faith. He should be certain that his so-called religious conviction is conviction indeed and not merely a projection of his ego and is not actually a case of pride or stubbornness, or both. On the other hand, it is also a tragedy for one partner with real spiritual depth to water down his faith to accommodate the spiritual dearth and emptiness of the other. The engagement period is the time for religious matters to be worked at and solved if at all possible. Remember it will be more difficult, not less, to agree after the marriage.

Several Possible Questions

How long should an engagement be? It is, of course, impossible for one answer to include every situation. Each couple is unique and each has a different background, interpretation of engagement, and approach to marriage. How long have you known each other previous to the engagement? Have you had any course in preparation for marriage? Have you undertaken any personality tests and discussed them together with a counselor? All of these will definitely affect the matter of how long your engagement should be.

Almost every survey shows there is a positive relationship between the length of the engagement and the stability of the marriage. On the other hand, we must realize that an engagement can last too long. The purpose of the engagement is that the two may, in perfect freedom, discuss intimate matters concerning all of the aspects of marriage. If the engagement is too long, an excessive amount of nervous tension may develop. Postponed marriage can be harmful. A couple may decide to sexually consummate the marriage during the engagement period and have regrets later. On the other hand, they can grow tired of waiting, become discouraged and lose interest in each other. While it is important to have an engagement period, it is also important once a couple has decided to marry that they do it—after a reasonable length of engagement, of course. A good suggestion is that an engagement should normally last as long as six months but probably not more than two years.

Should one who is engaged date anyone else? The immediate answer of most people to this question would be, "Absolutely not!" This would certainly be the case in most instances. On the other hand, some people feel there are times when it is permissible for a young person to continue dating if the couple is separated by distance. This may, it is suggested by some, be true among college students, where the man is in the armed service or where the two live in different cities. Many, however, feel that until a couple is ready to cease dating others, they should not regard their engagement as firmly established.

Although many writers suggest "recreational" dating as acceptable, in that it helps to relieve the strain of separation, this writer personally feels that one is not ready to be formally engaged unless he is ready to forego dating others. If one, however, feels that he must date others while engaged, some guidelines should be followed. The following are suggested: (1) The dating should be for recreation or convenience without a romantic interest in the other person. (2) The dating should, by all means, not be limited to one person exclusively. (3) The dating should always be with the full understanding and approval of one's fiancé. (4) The dating should never be expected to come up to the standards of enjoyment that one experiences in dating his "intended." In fact, one should be careful that unfavorable comparisons are not made.

How much should we tell the person we intend to marry about our previous love life? There are, of course, two extremes. One couple, engaged to be married, went one night each week to a quiet place where they could be alone and took turns telling each other their whole life story. They did not consider any detail too trivial. They told each other everything. Finally, there was nothing left to tell because they knew everything about each other. This may be a good idea. On the other hand, couldn't this be overdone? Wouldn't there be such a thing as telling so much there is nothing new to learn about each other after marriage? The other extreme, however, is to tell nothing. This is certainly unwise. During the engagement period a couple needs to learn about each other's background. A full and frank discussion is wise.

What about past indiscretions? This question arises constantly in letters to columnists who give advice. How much of one's previous love life should be revealed? Few people marry who have not had previous cases of infatuation and perhaps love. Unless that experience resulted in sexual relationships, it is best to say as little as possible about it. If there has been sexual involvement, this might be another matter. If a girl, for instance, has had a child out of wedlock, she probably should be frank with the man and tell him from the start. Even if she covered it up completely and no one but her family knew, it is doubtful if she could live with him a lifetime without finally being forced to tell him because of the pressure on her own mind. There is, on the other hand, nothing more disgusting than to have to listen to one tell about his or her previous romances. Most girls frankly do not care about their husband's previous girl friends. Someone has facetiously said that a man wants to be a girl's first love, but a girl is usually content to be a man's last love. This is probably an oversimplification and is too general to be completely dependable, but it has much truth. Be frank about the past, but be careful!

How seriously should we be concerned about our doubts?

Every engagement period is plagued by this shadow falling across its path. There are several reasons why doubts come. The engagement period is a time of frankness. Increasing familiarity causes the glamour to wear off. Disillusionment comes.

During the days of dating, two people usually idealize each other. They can see no faults in the image they have of their loved one. During engagement, however, they see each other realistically—"wart and all." This awakening can come as a shock. Another cause of doubt is that any engagement based on emotion will fluctuate. Love is not emotion only, but it does have an element of emotional content. An engaged person may wonder why he does not feel the same way all the time toward his intended companion. He thus asks whether or not he is really in love. Some doubting is, of course, nothing but fear of the future. A couple is looking forward to marriage which is a completely new experience for them. They know of others who have been successful. They wonder if they are adequate for the responsibilities of married life.

Every person must decide for himself as to whether he will share his doubts with the one he intends to marry. In all probability, however, the other will suspect his doubts. It is usually difficult for one to hide his anxieties from someone with whom he is involved emotionally. In fact, to try to hide your serious doubts may be harmful to the relationship. If doubts continue and grow greater, you probably should consult a minister or some other type of counselor. Remember, however, that he cannot tell you what you ought to do. He can help you clarify your problems in your own mind. He can explore courses of action and discuss your problem with you, but in the final analysis, you must make the decision. It may be that your doubts are not doubts of the other person but are doubts of your own ability. It may be a matter of your own maturity and your own willingness to commit yourself to another person.

Remember, love is not merely liking certain *qualities* in a certain person. It is more than that. It is loving the *person*. It is loving him or her with a love that endures even in spite of some unlovely or undesirable qualities. To love a person is to enter into a complete and unique relationship. It is not a matter of do I love this person enough. It is a matter of do I love this person. It is not a matter of do I love Jim more than I love Tom and if I do I will marry Jim. If not, I will marry Tom. If you are still comparing your love for two people, you are not ready to marry either. To love is to enter into a unique and exclusive relationship with one person. If one person loves another, then he should have no fear that he does not love him or her enough.

To get doubts out into the open is healthy. We must remember, however, that this will either strengthen the relationship or will end it. No neutral ground is possible. It is natural to hesitate when you stand on the threshold of such an important step as marriage. One should realize the seriousness of it. You must not ignore the uncertainty that comes because this may be a sign you should cancel the wedding. It does not, however, necessarily call for this decision. If you are mature people, and if you are in love and ready for marriage, you should face your doubts together. This period of doubt can serve as a foundation and stepping-stone for you to meet together other problems that life may hold for you.

Make It a Happy Time

Many more things could be said about this crucial period of preparation for marriage. One other important subject certainly needs to be discussed—that of how intimate should a couple be in sexual matters. In other words, "How far should they go in their love making during the engagement period?" This will be discussed in the next chapter.

This time in life should be a happy time—a time of coming to know each other in a growing relationship. Engagement is a time of transition from courtship in general to marriage in particular. It is the prelude to a good marriage. If a couple will take time during their engagement for serious study and creative thinking concerning the responsibilities of married life, there will be a much greater likelihood that they will have a happy home.

---

[1] (New York: Association Press, 1960), p. 122.

4 *You're Not Married Yet!*

A college student asked a question which, to him, was important. "If a boy and girl are in love and plan to be married, is it wrong for them to engage in sexual relations now, and if so, why?" The class was silent. They respected the professor, and yet many of them could probably identify with the student's question. The teacher paused and gave his deliberate answer. "Yes, it is wrong. Why? Because it is accepting one of the privileges of marriage without accepting the responsibility of marriage."

This chapter will discuss the matter of intimacy during the engagement period. How far should a couple go in expressing themselves physically during the time preceding their marriage?

It Is a Problem

Let us be honest about the matter. When two people are in love and plan to be married soon, they face a crisis in their courtship. New feelings are struggling for expression. There is a growing awareness of closeness and intimacy. The physical and emotional impulses and powers within us are strong. Within a short time, the two will give themselves to each other completely and without reserve. It is difficult to wait.

The problem is so pressing that many do not wait. Some couples who have abstained completely in all their previous courtships break down their convictions with the excuse, "We're in love . . . in spirit we've already been married . . . it's all right."

Although many types of surveys have been made, it is doubtful any true picture will ever be gained of how many married couples actually waited until after the wedding vows to consummate their marriage. Many girls have yielded to their fiancé's pleading. Others have been equally willing. Often, couples have "gone the limit" in the last few weeks without intending to do so. The period of engagement is one that leads to greater closeness and provides a transition to the physical intimacy of marriage. Every engaged couple must face the problem and make their decision of what they will do.

The Authoritarian Answer

If you accept the Bible as your guide, the answer is clear. To consummate a marriage physically, before the actual ceremony, is morally wrong. God has ordained sexual relations to be practiced within the framework of marriage. Either premarital or extramarital relations are sinful. Fornication is the term generally used for sexual relations between unmarried persons while adultery is used for extramarital relations. Both are condemned specifically by the Bible writers.

Christianity has historically accepted this position. So far as the writer knows, no orthodox Christian interpretation of marriage has ever approved of premarital sex activity. One author makes a striking observation concerning this subject. Based on his studies, he contends that chastity was the only new virtue that the Christian religion introduced into the world.

For many of us, the Bible is the final answer. We are like the old-timer who spoke of his faith with earnest conviction, "God said it. I believe it. That settles it." Abraham Lincoln had this same type of faith. He said, "I am profitably engaged in reading my Bible. If a man will take all of it that he can on reason and the rest on faith, he will live and die a better man." Many of us feel no intellectual inferiority or paucity when we simply say that we accept the biblical standard of morality concerning sex and marriage.

There Are Other Reasons

Let us, however, examine the matter further. Is a thing right because the Bible says so or does the Bible say so because it is right? Of course, both are true, but we are nearer to the heart of the truth when we say that the Bible approves an action because it is for man's good and condemns it because it is not best for man.

Lucy Freeman and Harold Greenwald have written an excellent book entitled *Emotional Maturity in Love and Marriage.* It has been called a frank, sensible, sound, modern approach to marriage. Both of these authors are entirely objective in their approach. They do not examine the various issues from the standpoint of biblical injunctions. Yet here is a striking statement from them: "The premature consummation of sex, that is, before a real relationship has been established, often prevents a man and a woman from becoming acquainted with each other." [1]

It is true that they were not speaking of exactly what we are discussing in this chapter, but a further word from them is significant. "Many authorities believe that an important part of love is the inhibition of sexual expression and that the unfulfilled sexual feelings add a strength and a dimension to love. Love, they say, needs to be built on many psychic fronts before the final intimacy occurs. It is like the frosting on a cake, added last, after the substance has been formed. Many of our conventions arise out of centuries of experience as to what is believed best for both man and society. The custom that couples restrain themselves from engaging in sexual intimacy before marriage is thus believed to be a wise one psychologically." [2]

Robert Capon reminds engaged couples, "Premarital intercourse is not the same thing as the marriage bed." He says, "Of course there is something unique about the first time whenever it comes, but if it comes before, there is inevitably attached to it the fillip of the forbidden." He continues, "It doesn't matter how enlightened people are, or how blasé the society is; our mores, honored in breach or observance, are our mores, and we're stuck with them. We might as well try to change our air. Do it now . . . and doing it later will have the edge taken off it to say the least." [3] Freeman and Greenwald agree, "The woman who breaks society's rules may experience a sense of guilt no matter how she may excuse what she does. The guilt will destroy much of her delight, both in the man and in the sexual intimacy. And, no matter how liberal intellectually the man or woman may be, there will often exist the erosive feeling that should the woman permit intimacy before marriage she is wanton. She may be thought of as 'a bad woman' both by her lover and herself because she could not control herself until they were legally bound to each other." [4]

Capon goes even further. He advises engaged couples not only to refrain from sexual intercourse but to do without all the "little semi-moral approximations to it: the petting that everybody takes for granted." He insists that doesn't help the situation one bit. He states that if there are worthwhile and pleasurable discoveries to be made by them, it would be much better to make them later amid a pile of unpaid bills where they could "lighten the load of lifelong monogamy." Even if one is not willing to approach morality from a Christian viewpoint, these reasons make good sense.

People Still Believe in Virtue

Many writers today are misleading young people in the matter of moral behavior. They are giving statistics on surveys and results of interviews which seem to indicate there are practically no boys or girls left who had not had sex experience before marriage. This simply is not true. There are many young people in high school, college, and at work who still believe in old-fashioned chastity—no sex relations before marriage.

It all depends on how the survey is taken. Some interviewers go about their work in such a way that practically the only people questioned are those who have already had sex experience and would like to convince the world that every young person is doing the same. Remember any college young girl interviewed who has had sex experience would like to convince the interviewer that every girl in the dormitory follows the same life-style.

Fair, unbiased, and objective polls, however, reveal that America still believes in Bible-based morals. In one recent survey, fifteen thousand individuals of all ages were questioned. Only 4 percent said yes when asked if premarital sexual relations are all right for engaged couples. Another survey, this one on the campus of a midwestern college, showed that 84 percent of the girls disagreed with the statement, "Premarital sex relations are all right for people who are engaged and going to be married." The one leading the survey summarized her findings: "Both parents and students appear to be more 'moral,' that is more frequently 'on the side of the angels,' than current discussions of the state of our society's morals would lead one to expect."

Evelyn Millis Duvall studied university freshmen girls on a number of campuses and found 88 percent disagreeing with the statement: "It is not important for a person to remain pure until marriage." She gives her conclusions, "Review of sex standards among today's young Americans leads to the conclusions that most men as well as women feel that abstinence before marriage is really best. . . . Everyone does not go in for premarital sexual activity. . . . In any school, college, or community there are enough of those who prefer to wait until marriage, so that a fellow or girl who wants to be one of them has plenty of company. The weight of the evidence is still on the side of chastity." [5]

You Must Decide!

This is your own personal choice. No one can make it for you. If you consummate your marriage during the engagement period, no one else but you two may ever know it. But you two will know it! Each of you will know that you are married to someone that was not willing to wait and you will lose an element of respect for that person as well as for yourself.

You want your marriage to be happy and successful. You will be wise if you decide deliberately in the beginning of your engagement that you will not go "all the way" before marriage. It might be a good policy to talk about it and set down some practical guidelines to keep your lovemaking within proper bounds. A marriage counselor once worked with a group of engaged couples in outlining the symptoms of when to stop and do something else. They came up with these practical suggestions: (1) when either is flushed and uncomfortable; (2) when either senses an urgency to continue the petting; (3) when either finds himself or herself restless and sleepless for extended periods after being together; (4) when the love play is an unpleasant memory with aspects of shame or guilt; (5) when being with the loved one is fun only when there are physical contacts. You may add your own to these.

Although William Shakespeare lived several centuries ago, he gives engaged couples good advice in the words he puts into the mouth of Prospero and Ferdinand. The father speaks to the young man concerning his daughter:

> Then, as my gift, and thine own acquisition
> Worthily purchased, take my daughter: but
> If thou dost break her virgin-knot before
> All sanctimonious ceremonies may
> With full and holy rite be ministered
> No sweet aspersion shall the heavens let fall
> To make this contract grow; but barren hate,
> Sour-eyed disdain and discord shall bestrew
> The union of your bed with weeds so loathly
> That you shall hate it both. . . .

Ferdinand replies:

> As I hope
> For quiet days, fair issue and long life,
> With such love as 'tis now, the murkiest den,

> The most opportune place, the strong'st suggestion
> Our worser genius can, shall never melt
> Mine honor into lust, to take away
> The edge of that day's celebration.

It's hard to improve on this philosophy even in our sophisticated twentieth century.

---

[1] Lucy Freeman and Harold Greenwald, *Emotional Maturity in Love and Marriage* (New York: Dell Publishing Co., Inc., 1961), pp. 14-15.

[2] *Ibid.*

[3] Robert Capon, *Bed and Board* (New York: Simon and Schuster, 1965), p. 23.

[4] *Op. cit.,* p. 15.

[5] Evelyn Millis Duvall, *Why Wait Till Marriage* (New York: Association Press, 1965), pp. 22-23.

5　Getting the Marriage Started Right

Centuries ago a Greek philosopher said, "The beginning is half the whole." Another student wrote, "We shut our eyes to the beginnings of evil because they are small, and in this weakness lies the germ of our defeat. . . . This maxim closely followed would preserve us from almost all our misfortunes." A French scholar wrote, "The first step, my son, which one makes in the world, is the one on which depends the rest of our days."

None of these men were referring to marriage in their statements, but all of them apply with a striking relevance. One of the most important factors in assuring a happy married life is to be certain it gets "off the ground" without misunderstandings or scars. One husband confessed how startled he was, after more than twenty years of marriage, when his wife told him how much she still resented an unthoughtful act of his during the first few days of their marriage. It pays to get started right!

Have a Meaningful Wedding

This does not mean the wedding must be an expensive one. Some of the costliest weddings are the "corniest" and the crudest, while some of the most economical are the most dearly remembered. There are few, if any, times when a "runaway wedding" is advisable. A young couple owes it to their parents to allow them the privilege of being present. There will be enough adjustments in the bringing together of two families without having either one, or both, resent the fact they were not told of the plans or invited to the wedding.

Should the wedding be by a religious official or by a civil one? Historically, religious ceremonies are far more numerous. First marriages, and couples belonging to the same faith, more often have religious ceremonies. Also, rural brides, younger brides and grooms, and grooms who are farmers or professional men fall into this category. Divorced people, older couples, and those of different religious faiths tend to have civil ceremonies. There has been, in recent years, a slight tendency away from marriage by religious officials.

This step is too important, however, to be completely secularized. Nor is there any likelihood that it will be. Religion is still too deeply ingrained in our national and personal life to be separated from the marriage vows by the majority of the people. We will have to go much farther down the road to complete secularization and be much more "sophisticated" to eliminate the desire of most young couples to marry within the framework of a religious setting. Even the sourest cynic finds it difficult to agree that the time may come when the official pronouncement of the clergyman, the orange blossoms, the white bridal gown, the voice that breathed o'er Eden, the "oohs and ahs" as favors are distributed, and the formal reception will be quaint social survivals of backward areas. Marriage is an institution of God. As long as we have it, we will seek God's approval.

Why have a meaningful wedding? All girls, and even seemingly nonchalant men, love to look back to the beautiful experience. Marriage counselors testify that a couple in domestic difficulty will usually sparkle and become soft when they talk about their wedding. To get the marriage started right, have a meaningful ceremony.

A Private and Happy Honeymoon

Much has been written about the requirements for an ideal

honeymoon. Yet, many counselors advise delaying the honeymoon until later when the couple have come to know each other better. A well-known playwright and novelist says: "Think of the fatal consequences when two strange human beings of different habits built up for many years and of totally different environments who are not yet fully acquainted with each other's manner and ways, go away alone with no other plan in mind but to see each other continuously and shut out every acquaintance and friend. Let me assure you that it's a far more difficult trial of endurance than any other I can think of and an extremely dangerous one." It has been suggested that the couple should go away for three or four days and then come back to work and begin planning their home and homelife together. The joy of the first lovely days of marriage are then experienced in the home.

This idea has merit, but each couple will make its own decision. Most feel that the honeymoon is designed to meet specific needs and should not be postponed. Two hazards should be avoided. The first is excessive cost, and the other is overfatigue. Either one can cause friction which will put scars on the marriage early in its existence. Privacy is an important part of the honeymoon. You should select a place where this is guaranteed. Hotel arrangements should be made in advance.

Another word of caution is wise. Do not expect too much from the honeymoon. Some have been disappointed because they have anticipated great thrills from the first sex relationship. The early experiences may be awkward and clumsy. Remember also that there will be disillusionments. Prolonged intimacy with each other will bring out problems of adjustments in personal hygiene, sensory details of bodily functions, and differing opinions of habits with reference to use of bathroom facilities. The word "disillusionment" may sound like an ugly word. Perhaps a better expression would be "facing realities."

A marriage is much more likely to be started right if the

honeymoon is a pleasant experience. Couples will do well to remember this and work toward making the first nights together moments of thoughtfulness and unselfishness. Don't be disturbed if there is a discrepancy between what you have imagined the honeymoon will be and what it actually is. Each one should work to help the period be a source of joy and happiness for the other.

An Understanding About Children

A recent story, in a popular magazine, told of a family in Connecticut which was discussing planned parenthood. The young son heard them talking and suddenly chipped in his idea, "Oh, I think planned parenthood is a very good idea. I can think of several things about my parents that could have been better planned." Whether we agree with it or not, the importance and even necessity for planned parenthood is here to stay. A young couple will do well to face this matter early in its wedded life.

How soon do you want a family? The old feeling, and it seems to still be a good one, was, "enjoy each other for at least the first year." Unless a couple has postponed marriage for a number of years and is anxious to have children, it is probably not their desire for the girl to come back from the honeymoon pregnant. There should be a frank discussion and definite decision about how soon children are wanted.

Of course, planning is not always successful. The couple many times becomes careless and the first child is a "slip." Caution for the first few months, however, is possible and will usually be effective. To give any firm guidelines as to how soon a couple should have children would be presumptious. Conditions vary. The point is that it should be discussed and each should respect the wishes of the other. If there is a disagreement, a compromise should be reached that is satisfactory to both. This is extremely important in getting the marriage started right.

A Sensible Budget

Young couples today face the most confused financial picture of our century. Salaries are higher than ever but so are prices and taxes. The purchasing power of the dollar has declined continuously since 1946 and drastically the last few years. Added to this is the fact that pressures for higher living standards grow stronger and stronger. Many middle-aged couples are only now beginning to buy some of the things for their home that young couples seem to feel they must have the first years of their married life.

Even before marriage a couple should have already discussed their financial program. In the early days of wedded life some decisions will have to be made. Will the financial program be such that every dollar earned will already be obligated by payday? Will you live from paycheck to paycheck or will you adopt some long-range goals? Unless a sensible approach to finances is adopted, a young couple can get into an economic crisis the first year that can penalize them five years in their financial programming.

Of course, everyone is different. Some couples do not mind indebtedness. Others are terrified by it. The wise couple, however, will refrain from wanting all the luxuries immediately. Save something to look forward to with anticipation. Most of the fun of a trip or any joyful experience is looking forward to it. So the same with lovely furniture or any extra conveniences for the home. Economic instability is at the root of many, we might even say most, marriage difficulties. Get the marriage started right with sensible financial planning.

A Separate Home

Some of the clichés are still good. That is why we call them "truisms." They are true in every generation. One of the oldest says, "No kitchen is big enough for two women." Likewise, no home is big enough for two families. It is the unanimous verdict of all counselors, "When you become married, get into your own home."

It doesn't have to be a big house. It can be a small apartment with merely a kitchenette. But it is yours! If you want to put scars on the marriage that may never heal, go to live with your in-laws. They may be lovely, kind, generous, and sympathetic. They may want to be helpful, but you will be better off in a separate house—preferably on a different street, or even better still, in a different neighborhood.

Worship Together

Every survey taken shows a definite relationship between worshiping together and staying happily married. This does not mean that every couple who goes to church and is active in it is free from problems and sometimes even divorce. Not at all! The evidence, however, is overwhelming that the more dedicated a couple is to their church, and the more vital their religious life together, the greater the likelihood the marriage will be stable and their emotional life secure.

Even on the honeymoon, or rather we might say "especially on the honeymoon," go to a worship service together. If you are of the same faith, so much the better. Statistics show the chances for your marriage's success are increased from the beginning. If you are of different faiths, don't joke about your companion's religion or denomination. Feelings can be hurt over words spoken in jest. Remember, most people who "joke with a dig" really mean the dig. And the other knows it! Early scars can last a long time.

If anyone ever needed to pray together, it is a young couple starting their life together. One testified from years of observation,

"I've never known divorce to break a home
Where a man and woman pray,
Kneeling together by their fireside at the close of day,
Or reading in the early morning there,

God's Word to help them through
The hours ahead. I have never known divorce
To break such homes—have you?"
But you must begin early if it becomes a habit of life. Such
thinking as this may seem terribly archaic and slightly "square"
to some young couples today. When we look at the rapidly rising
divorce rate, however, and see the number of people rushing
desperately to marriage counselors and others for professional
help because of their domestic difficulties, when the cry of today
is "Can this marriage be saved?" we might stop and ask ourselves
a question. Is it not just quite possible, even probable, that these
so-called "squares" of another day knew more about the real
meaning of life than our present generation does with its lax
and permissive attitudes and the sophistication that is so preva-
lent and accepted. If you want to start the marriage right, learn
to worship together!

Watch Little Things

When the honeymoon fades and the reality of day-to-day
living sets in, problems begin to arise. If there has been any
deep-seated conflict in one's personality before marriage, it will
become highly intensified as wedded life begins. The early weeks
and months of marriage are the time to be exceedingly careful
about annoying habits and wrong attitudes—the little foxes that
spoil the vineyard.

The young married couple should watch their words. Unkind
things said about each other's family during this period are
difficult, almost impossible, to forgive. If a husband speaks even
in jest about a habit of his bride, he can hurt her deeply—so
the same with a wife to a husband. Each one is feeling frightened
and insecure in the new role and relationship. Be careful with
your tongue. Will Carleton in *First Settlers Story* said:

> Boys flying kites haul in their white-winged birds
> You can't do that way when you're flying words!

> Careful with fire is good advice we know
> Careful with words is ten times doubly so.
> Thoughts unexpressed may sometimes fall back dead,
> But God Himself can't kill them once they're said!

One lady, saddened by a recent experience of talking too much, admitted to a group:

> I'm careful of the words I say
> To make them nice and sweet
> I never know from day to day
> Which ones I'll have to eat.

There are other little things to watch. Don't become careless about being polite. A husband should continue to open the door for his wife. He should notice the way she dresses and compliment her on her appearance. To change slightly the words of a once popular song, "Stay as sweet as you were."

Learn to Speak the Same Language

Free and open communication is necessary in order for two people to love each other completely. A husband and wife should share each other's inner joys and sorrows, hopes and fears. There is only one way to accomplish this goal. You must know each other—what your companion thinks, feels, and does—and even more important you need to know why—if you are to find fulfillment in your life together.

Early in their togetherness, a couple should learn to be honest with each other. This begins by being honest with oneself. Neither of these is easy. All of our prewedded life we have been accustomed to denying and repressing our true feelings. A boy learns early in life that if he cries or in any way shows that he has been hurt, he will be labeled as a "sissy." In fact, any expressions of doubt or anxiety on a boy's part of his ability to achieve can earn him the reputation of being a weakling. Thus boys learn early to disguise any feeling of inadequacy. Girls perhaps do not feel this pressure so greatly, but they learn

early also there are times when it is better to keep quiet lest
they be considered aggressively unfeminine.

It is difficult, when one becomes married, to suddenly begin
communicating with another person the feelings we have kept
secret, even buried, for many years. Yet it is in such communication that a bride and groom come to know and adjust
to each other. A husband and wife should sit down and discuss
intelligently, without either feeling threatened, anything and
everything that is of mutual interest and concern, creates anxiety,
causes fear, raises doubt, or produces any serious or unhealthy
emotions. They should especially communicate about their ex-
pectations and the role each desires to play in the relationship.
This will enable them to bring to the surface any differing
concepts which might be present. The fewer subjects which a
couple puts beyond the bounds of discussion and the fewer areas
they avoid in order to keep from rocking the boat, the fuller
and more complete the relationship will be.

Young couples should learn early that there is more to communication than dialogue with each other. Of course, talking
is one way to reveal to another what we are thinking, but it
is possible to conceal our inner thoughts even while speaking.
Often in nagging or criticizing, the thing we say is not the real
reason for our irritating condemnation. Talking is effective and
fruitful only if it accurately represents our inner feelings. Actually, we can communicate with a glance or with that most
annoying and exasperating of all approaches, "the silent treat-
ment." Communication in marriage is keeping in touch with
each other's heart secrets. In this way, each of you knows what
is going on inside. It is the dynamic process between husband
and wife as they ask for information, being sure to give and
receive responses. This assures that each one understands what
the other is thinking and feeling.

Make the Right Kind of Friends

Although you will enjoy each other solely and uninterruptedly for a while, this blissful monopoly will soon begin to wane. Not that you will necessarily become tired of each other, but you will want friends to share your social life.

What kind of friends? You will soon discover that you have practically nothing in common with your single associates. Age doesn't matter. If you are twenty-two and twenty, you will have more in common with two eighteen-year-olds who are married or two thirty-five-year-olds that are married than with a couple your own age who are not yet committed to each other in matrimony. Don't fight it! Join it! Make friends among the married people. You are now one of them.

Your social life will have a great influence on your marriage. If you are still in school, your budget will circumscribe your social affairs and, to a large extent, determine your friends. In all probability, your best friends will be the new couples you meet after marriage. With America becoming increasingly mobile (one out of every four families moves every year), you will not be likely to retain friendships from your courting days. Many new couples live, for a year or two, in an apartment. This means new acquaintances.

How much partying will you do? How much can you afford? How permissive are your ideas in social activities? Do you want friends who are Christians and church related or do you want to give church a respectable nod on Sunday morning and forget it the rest of the week or for several weeks? Questions such as these will help shape the path of the early marriage years. When a young man, destined to become one of the outstanding ministers of history, enrolled at Oxford, he made a statement that young married couples might consider. He said, "I will have no friends that do not help me on the road to being a better Christian." Newly married couples need friends that will give strength and stability, not the kind who will add to their problems. Elizabeth Barrett Browning once asked Charles Kingsley, "Tell me the secret of your life that I, too, may make mine beautiful." He replied, "I had a friend." If you have the proper kind of friends, you can get the marriage started right.

Most marriages that end up in divorce court had the beginning of their trouble in the early years. When the missile climbs off the launching pad correctly, it has an excellent chance making it into orbit correctly and functioning effectively. So it is with a marriage!

---

[1] (Waco: Word Books, 1968), p. 13.

[2] New York: Harper & Brothers, 1953), p. 61.

[3] Rudolf Besier, *The Barretts of Wimpole Street* (Boston: Little, Brown and Co., 1958), p. 105.

6   *Pacing Yourself for the Long Haul*

One disillusioned cynic, with his tongue in cheek, criticized the marriage ceremony: "When two people are under the influence of the most violent, most insane, most delusive, and most transient of passions, they are required to solemnly swear they will remain in that excited, abnormal, and exhausting condition continuously until death do them part." As we all know—it simply can't be done! Marriage, like life itself, is not a snapshot—it is a time exposure.

If a marriage is to live, it must, like all living things, grow and develop. A weary woman once said, "Life is so daily." So is marriage. In fact, marriage is about the most daily thing to be found. Men sometimes complain, "Too many girls think a woman's work is done when she sweeps down the aisle." Or "A pretty girl is like a melody—after you marry her you have to face the music." Women, on the other hand, often feel like complaining:

> Breakfast, my love, with me gaily
>   Make it apparent what pleasure,
> What joy you consider it daily
>   To commune with a wife who's a treasure.
>
> Let love be a flame that burns brightly
>   Instead of a flickering taper,
> Dear heart, converse with me lightly—
>   Or pass me some part of that paper!

There is more to marriage than "getting it started right." We must settle down for the long haul and face some issues honestly and with a firm resolve to make our marriage not merely a fifty-yard dash but a cross-country run.

It Won't Be Perfect

When a couple is in love, they usually dream of "absolutes" as they contemplate their marriage. They believe it will be an ideal relationship. To them, wedded life will be free of all the mistakes and imperfections they have seen in other marriages. Somehow, in their romantic fantasy, they are sure perfect harmony will exist, and there will never be arguments to disrupt the atmosphere of their love. In short, their life together will be a never-ending honeymoon.

Such people are in for a rude awakening! At the beginning of her book, *Good Marriages Grow,* Irene Harrell says, "My husband isn't perfect—thank goodness! If he were, I would feel horribly guilty about saddling him with me. I seem to have missed perfection by a few billion light-years myself." Mrs. Harrell goes on to say, however, that they have had an unbelievably happy marriage for nearly fourteen years in spite of their imperfections. In fact, she suggests that maybe their happiness was because of their mutual imperfections.[1] In the arts it is the "striving toward perfection" which brings zest to life. Should it not be also with the fine art of marriage? To grow together, through the years in a rewarding and fulfilling marriage, is essentially a work of art among human relationships. The surest way to achieve genuine and lasting joy in wedded life is to realize from the beginning that marriage does not create a static relationship between two people, but rather one of mutual and interactive growth.

There will probably be mild disagreements, and perhaps arguments, even during the early weeks and months of marriage. It may be a year or so, even longer, however, before serious crises begin to occur. Just as in the early weeks of marriage neither should run home to mother and dad, likewise when the more serious crises of marriage come they must be faced with maturity and calm acceptance of the fact that as "every home has its hush," so every marriage is imperfect.

You and your companion must work at the job of having a happy life together. There will, of course, be errors. We should be prepared to accept the fact that mistakes are not only an acceptable part of life—they are essential to a full life. Without the intelligent use of our mistakes, we would never go on to master any skill. This is doubly true about marriage. It takes a sense of humor to admit our mistakes and laugh at ourselves, but when we can do it we have achieved wisdom. A wise man, after many years of experience with life, said, "Finish each day and be done with it. You have done what you could. Some blunders and absurdities no doubt crept in; forget them as soon as you can. Tomorrow is a new day; begin it well and serenely, and with too high a spirit to be cumbered with your old non-sense." Your marriage won't be perfect. Don't expect it to be!

Decide on Long-range Goals

What do you really want out of marriage? In fact, what do you want out of life itself? Is your overwhelming obsession to have material success and accumulate an abundance of things which will give you complete financial security? Is your biggest desire in life for a career? Is the thing you really want a certain standard of living? Is it your supreme desire to have a family and give your best to the rearing of children? Is your chief aim in life and in marriage to be socially prominent—to entertain frequently and successfully?

Few people ever analyze themselves and try to answer such questions as these, and fewer still ever discuss them with their companion. Unless one knows how he feels about such questions and unless a husband and wife face these matters candidly, they are seriously handicapped as they settle down for a long and happy marriage.

A marriage cannot be happy and successful to the fullest unless each member helps the other to meet his emotional needs. If a couple finds satisfaction through each other, they can feel secure and unified against the world. Their being together enables them to face courageously both the old and new anxieties of living. Sexual satisfaction is, of course, important but this alone cannot meet all of the emotional needs. On the other hand, the lack of complete sexual adjustment does not necessarily mean that a marriage will be entirely unhappy. There are many more emotional needs in life than merely one's sexual desires. A part of long-range planning is to recognize each other's emotional needs and face them realistically.

A couple must also approach financial problems as partners. They must trust each other. They must decide early in marriage to consult each other concerning the present and the future as they plan for expenditures and for possible investments. It is wise to plan an insurance program in the early years of marriage. Too often, a man does not think of insurance until several children have come. Actually, the earlier he begins his insurance program, the cheaper the rates. Insurance should be taken on the breadwinner of the family first. If a couple can discipline themselves early in their marriage to begin their insurance program, they should come to middle age well provided for in this area.

Investments in stocks and bonds are good, but all counselors in this field advise a couple to work out their insurance program satisfactorily before they start in an investing program. The writer remembers several people whom he has known and their experiences might be helpful at this point.

There was a man who had three children. He boasted that he had all the insurance on his children—none on himself. He said, "I love my children and I want the insurance to be on them." Actually, he was alarmingly overweight himself and if he had passed away suddenly, his wife and family would have had no protection. While it is a good thing to take a policy out on a child, if one can afford it, it is far better to insure the father so the wife and children can be beneficiaries in case of his death.

Another man went to an investment broker to talk about some investments. The first thing the broker asked him was concerning his insurance program. When it was found that he had little or no insurance, the broker said, "I would like very much to buy stock for you, but the first thing for you to do is to go see a good insurance man and get sufficient coverage for your wife and family."

One of the most amusing incidents the writer remembers is that of a relatively young professor. He wanted some stocks because many of his colleagues were investing. He had no money so he cashed in one of his insurance policies upon which he had paid for a number of years. He took the cash value and invested it in stock. He explained, "I wanted to be able to join in the conversation at social gatherings as to the stock market and what investments I had." Needless to say, the man wasted good money by forfeiting protection for his family.

One of the first things a couple should do is to make a will. There may be differences of opinion concerning joint bank accounts or joint budgeting, but there can be no difference of opinion about a joint will. A good lawyer should be consulted and his advice taken. Even though one's assets are limited, they will grow and become more complex through the years. A will, properly written, may save a headache and also money in case of the death of either partner.

A health program is a part of long-range planning. A family should have a good medical doctor in whom they have confidence and with whom they can maintain a good relationship through the years. The old slogan, "See your dentist at least twice a year," is still a good one. Dental work done early is far more economical and protects the teeth as well. Maintaining good health is vital to every area of married life.

Two Yet One

What happens to individuality in marriage as the years go by? What should happen? Is the ideal of marriage that two should become one? It is certainly true that Jesus said, "The two shall become one flesh." Someone has described the ideal marriage as a mingling of two lives so intimately that their individual lives are thereafter indistinguishable. Theodore F. Adams in *Making Your Marriage Succeed* quotes a wife as saying, "Life has taught us that love does not consist in gazing at each other, but in looking outward together in the same direction." Adams says, "There is no comradeship except from union in the same high effort, that is the building of a Christian home." [2]

Certainly, marriage is a blending of two personalities into one. As the years go by the strength of one will supplement the weakness of the other. Perhaps women learn to do this better than men. The wife is usually more conscious of her need to be a good companion and "stand in the gap" by compensating for the place where her husband is deficient. If a man is a strong "extrovertish" personality who is in danger of ruffling people by his extreme zeal and "pushiness," the wife will probably learn early in marriage to be the sweet quiet personality to compensate for her husband's aggressiveness. On the other hand, some men are naturally passive, and the wife feels she must be the one who pushes. Someone has said that often marriage is a union between masculine strength and feminine loveliness.

Do you remember the passage in *The Barretts of Wimpole Street* where Elizabeth complains concerning her inadequacies? She says, "I love you too well to let you waste your manhood pursuing the pale ghost of a woman." Robert Browning replies, "I tell you, in all soberness, that my need of you is as urgent as your need of me. If your weakness asks my strength for support, my abundant strength cries out for your weakness to complete my life and myself." [3] Marriage is indeed the blending of mutual strengths and weaknesses into one beautiful whole.

But is this the full story? Is there not a need for us to see that each should be left free in marriage to develop his own personality to the fullest? One of the great problems in this computer age is that we have lost our sense of being an individual. The man at the factory or office feels the threat of being replaced by an impersonal machine. For many years, however, the wife and mother has felt that her individual personality has been buried beneath the maze of housework and tending to children. Although we may hesitate to accept all the contentions of the "avant garde" thinkers of the modern movements for women's rights, we certainly can agree strongly that the woman should have both opportunity and encouragement to develop her personality also.

For one thing, the woman is better educated today than she was a generation ago. More housewives and mothers have college degrees. A woman easily becomes not only frustrated but bored to death when she feels that she has ceased to develop as an individual. It is for this reason that many counselors are advising the woman to find a place in the world beyond her home.

There will be disagreement concerning this advice. But the point is, and it is a point well taken, that although two become one they still remain two personalities. The man in today's world cannot exploit or dominate the woman to such a degree that she becomes devoid of her own personality. The "enslavement of the personal" does not develop character or personality in the other. It cannot be the basis for long-range success and happiness in the married life. Each partner in a marriage should seek to develop the wisdom that enables him to help the other become and remain a person—in all that the term implies. This is a vital part of the long pull in marriage.

The alarming divorce rate today frightens us, and there are many reasons for it. One counselor, however, gives us an interesting and provocative observation. He says that we overlook the fact that a generation or two ago women were virtually

dependent upon their husbands. They were not prepared to go
out into the world and make a living. If their homelife was
unhappy, they were "stuck with it." This is not the case today.
For this reason, many more women go to the divorce court and
seek to be relieved from an unhappy marriage.

Beyond a doubt, if we knew the truth, there were just as many
unhappy marriages on the farm, and in the cities as well, two
generations ago as today, but women were not able to assert
their individuality. This writer has recently composed a new
marriage ceremony in which part of the vow is that each promises
to help the other develop as a person. This is a far cry from
the old idea that the woman is to be "obedient unto the husband
in all things." The two should indeed be one, but they also
should remain two, and a wise couple will recognize this as
they face the years of companionship before them.

Marriage Can Be Fun

It's always dangerous to oversimplify, but if one element stands
above all others in pacing ourselves, it is that we learn to develop
a real sense of humor in marriage. There is much indeed that
we can laugh about! When a wife and husband are so secure
in their love for each other that they can kid about the ordinary
things of marriage, they are well on the road to success. You
simply cannot stay on the mountaintop of romantic love all the
time. The daily drudgeries come. Couples need to laugh at
themselves and their problems.

Part of married life is a man being able to kid his wife. One
man described a female shopper as a woman "who can hurry
through a department store aisle eighteen inches wide without
brushing against the piled-up glassware, and then drive home
and knock the doors off a twelve-foot-wide garage." This man
found great delight in reading an advertisement in a newspaper
that said, "If your wife wants to drive, don't stand in her way."
One wife, on the other hand, loves to kid her husband,

> The Watts are at their ten room shack
> On salty Buzzards Bay,
> Since June the Murphys have enjoyed
> Their pseudo-Swiss chalet.
>
> The Angneys, Briggs and Bumps are at
> Their breezy lakeside lodges
> The Cooks are at their country house—
> So are the Henry Hodges.
>
> We, too, are at our summer place—
> We really have some balls here,
> But here's our gripe: We also spend
> Our winters, springs, and falls here!

The matter of money will always be a problem in marriage. Someone has described marriage as "oceans of emotions surrounded by expanses of expenses." Why not learn to joke about money and the tight budget. In most quips it is the man who is complaining about the wife who is a big spender. This is not always true, but it seems to get the laughs. One man with a tremendous income is reported to have given as the reason for his success, "I have been trying to find some income beyond which my wife cannot live." That often leads us to joke,

> Spending money, much to
> my chagrin,
> Is what I seldom have when
> she has been.

and smile understandingly at the "helpful hints for husbands"

> Don't give her hose or fancy clothes
> For fear you'll miss her size:
> Don't try to pick some little trick
> To help her glamorize:
> There's one suggestion, you'll agree,
> That's sure to be a honey:
> Just give her love and compliments—
> Gift wrapped in rolls of money.

Learn to laugh at each other and together at the matter of finances. You'll be glad.

The matter of communication in marriage is important. A psychologist who directs the marriage counseling training program at one of our nation's outstanding mental health clinics, says, "Lack of communication is the big problem in marriages today. Too many couples have lost the art of talking it over. I'd rather see a husband and wife argue, even heatedly, than see one of them go silent and walk out of the room." This dialogue entertained a group recently. It is a tongue-in-cheek treatise on "The Fine Art of Marital Conversation":

> I'm always reading the questionaires in the paper to find out if I have a happy marriage.
>
> This one asks, "Wives, are you failing your husbands? Has your marriage become humdrum because you can discuss nothing but petty household problems?"
>
> After twenty years, most of our conversation is about household problems, so I could easily see I was failing my husband.
>
> It is never too late to change. I picked up a trade journal to find a few interesting topics of conversation to spring on my bored husband.
>
> At breakfast I bubbled vivaciously, "Good morning, dear! Do you think the Twelve-Speed Spicer is better than other transmissions?"
>
> My husband looked at me as if I had lost my marbles and replied, "I don't know, I never had one. Did you get the oil changed?"
>
> I hadn't, and we were back on petty household problems.
>
> I'm not easily discouraged. At dinner we could have an interesting political discussion.
>
> "Wasn't the governor's message interesting?" I asked, as my husband was sipping his coffee.
>
> "Not half as interesting as the message I'll have if the kids don't get those bicycles out of the driveway!" he growled.
>
> "Tell me, dear," I inquired after the kids were in bed, "do

you think an open training camp is better for a fighter than a closed training camp?"

"It depends on the fighters," answered my husband. "You'd better go into training if you don't get the buttons sewn on my shirt."

From now on I shall keep my conversation on petty household problems like, "When are you going to fix that leaky faucet?" or "How do you expect the kids to pick up their things when you leave your shoes in the middle of the living room?"

I may be a bore, but I've been in training long enough to know the offensive fighter wins the points.

Perhaps the best advice for communication in marriage is given by Ogden Nash,

> To keep your marriage brimming
> With love and the loving cup,
> Whenever you are wrong, admit it;
> Whenever you are right, shut up.

Humor in marriage is important. It is probably one of the best signs of a happy family. It has been called "the sunshine of the mind." Many husbands and wives can get out of the deadlock of petty quarrels by wisecracking, repartee, or a good joke. Laughter may be a lifesaver. As we develop a sound sense of humor, we shall recognize some of the absurdities of our cranky ideas and pompous postures without becoming cynical about them. It is difficult to see how two people can live together comfortably over a long period of time if they do not know how to have fun and to laugh.

Practical Matters

One of marriage's eternal problems is that of the *in-laws*. They can be helpful or they can be the greatest enemy of one's marriage. Usually, though not always, the problem will be the mother who cannot give up a son and the father who cannot give up a daughter. The more mature one is in his own emotional life, the more apt he is to have patience with immature in-laws who insist on dominating the marriage. There is no one solution to the matter which answers all situations. A couple should remember, however, that if they do not wish to be taken advantage of by unexpected and uninvited visits from in-laws, they should not open the door to it by expecting to impose on the older generation for every advantage which can be exploited. It's a two-way track, and if you want a long happy life with your in-laws, don't expect any more from them than you are willing to give to them by way of special privileges.

Who will handle the *money?* Face the matter realistically! Which one is better qualified? One thing is certain. The financial aspect of your marriage must be a family partnership. You must be able to discuss frankly with each other how much each of you earns, if both are working. You must also discuss your hopes for saving. You should be entirely honest with each other.

You might consider these suggestions which have been made for married people:

1. Set up two bank accounts—one a checking account and the other a savings account. Make both of them joint accounts.

2. Divide the responsibility for paying bills. Perhaps the husband should write the checks for such items as rent, mortgage, insurance, etc. The wife, on the other hand, could keep track of and pay the bills for food, entertainment at home, etc. Balance your books once a month, preferably together.

3. If the wife works and must pay household expense, part of her paycheck should probably be used at this point.

4. If you plan to begin a family soon, save a large part of the wife's paycheck from the very beginning. This will speed the nest egg. It also will partially prepare you for living on only one paycheck.

5. List your fixed, unavoidable expenses for a complete year.

Put aside some money each month to provide for these future payments. This will avoid a crisis when the bills come due.

6. Decide on a personal allowance for each one of you. Let this be each one's own affair as to how he spends it.

7. Plan your installment buying together. Make certain that even if an emergency comes you will have the capacity to repay without delay or penalty. Never take on an installment debt without agreeing on it together.

8. Consider your savings as a "fixed expense" which must be met even as other expenses are met. You cannot save "what's left over." It will never be there.

9. Periodically, reexamine and reevaluate your financial plan so as to make it even better. Do not attempt this, however, when you are in a frantic mood about money and likely to blow up.

Quite often a husband or wife will resent the other's *previous friends*. For instance, one wife had a girl friend who was constantly talking about their previous "double dates" before the wife met her husband. This irritated the husband. The wife realized it and wisely arranged to meet her girl friend away from home. In fact, she gradually weaned herself away from the girl because she realized that her presence made her husband uncomfortable. Sometimes old friendships may be compatible with marriage. Certainly an effort should be made to learn to appreciate and make room for the other's friends. If a friendship can be carried over into marriage, it can be rewarding for it provides a continuity between single life and married life through shared memories and new experiences.

We should, however, face the fact that the friends must have in common a similar attitude toward the person they both love in their different ways. The problem is, however, that we usually meet each other's friends during the period of courtship. We rarely, if ever, share one another's enthusiasm for friends each has known a long time. There is even an element of jealousy in one's reaction to a fiancé's old friends. Once the priority of marital claims is established some of this feeling may disappear. It is unreasonable, however, to expect that a husband or wife will ever experience an equal enthusiasm for friends acquired solely by marriage. This seldom, if ever, happens. A wise couple will recognize this truth and act accordingly.

A final practical suggestion concerns *togetherness* in marriage. Even if two people love each other dearly and are happy together, they occasionally need separations from each other. This enables them to gain new perspective and recreate their individuality. Too much intimacy without any interruptions can cause a marriage to "go stale."

When a fresh view of things is gained, one is usually eager to resume the intimacy of marriage and perfectly willing to assume the adjustments that are necessary from time to time. A night out with the boys or a day off to browse leisurely through the stores may be the very safety valve that is needed to let off the accumulated steam that has developed. It does not lead to division, but rather it helps a man or woman to retain his individuality—the thing which attracted them to each other originally. By no means should either partner expect the other to give a complete report of everything done every minute of every day. It is too much as though the person is not trusted. It comes from excessive insecurity on the part of the one who wants to know everything. Rather than bind the person closer to him, it can produce the opposite effect and drive the companion away. Love, understanding, and trust tie people together. An occasional holiday from marriage is practical and can be very profitable.

Capability to Love Grows

A man who had been married more than twenty years once said, "When I married my wife, I loved her with all of my heart. Yet, now that we have been married more than twenty years, I love her far more today than I did the day we married." Is this possible? Is there such a thing as "more than all"? If a man loves a woman with all of his heart, how can he later love her more than that? The answer is simple. His capacity for love increases.

Marriage is a continuing challenge. It does not "begin at the zenith of love with no direction to go but downward." It is not as one skeptic has described it "a meal with the dessert first." Actually, real love at the altar is not so much a fact as a possibility. It begins to grow and thrive with the years together. One woman who had been married for twenty years said to some friends, "And to think we believed we knew all about love the day we got married!"

In order for love to grow, each must seek to be genuinely interested in the other. This means more than merely telling the companion, "I love you." It means also seeking by the things we *do* to make the person realize we love him. A man should realize that a woman shows love to him, not only in the giving of herself physically, but in washing the dishes, doing the laundry, and cleaning the house. Love is not something you say to each other, it is something you do for each other. A marriage should not stand still. It should grow. It will grow if each seeks to become a helper for the other.

> Success in marriage, I have heard,
>   Does not depend so much
> On *finding* the right person
>   As it does on *being* such.

On the other hand, a wife must not think that doing all the chores around the house will substitute for a warm personal embrace and genuine physical affection for her husband.

> You can have your welcome *mat*
>   I ask a little more,
> When I come home from work I want
>   A welcome *mate* inside my door.

Robert Rainey, a prominent churchman, was facing much

criticism and general misunderstanding. A friend noticed how he could bear up under it. He asked Rainey how it could be done. Rainey replied, "Ah, you see, I'm very happy at home!"

There is a genuine security which comes when we know that our marriage is being enriched in the soil of love and that this love is making our marriage grow. We must remember constantly that love is a matter of giving, although we too often think of it as merely one of taking. Rather than asking one in the marriage ceremony, "Do you take this person?" perhaps we should ask, "Do you give yourself to this person?" This would probably prevent such a statement as one woman is reported to have made concerning her marriage. She said, "When I was married to him, we were both in love with him. I fell out of love with him but he didn't." If each gives to the other to help the marriage grow, neither will fall out of love with the other.

Settle Down

To have a marriage that lasts for years with reasonable happiness is not easy. Masterpieces come only with toil and hard work. To produce one takes, as someone said, "10 percent inspiration and 90 percent perspiration." A happy, lasting marriage requires the same work as that of producing a masterpiece. Indeed, this is what it is. Settle down. Rome wasn't built in a day. Neither will your marriage be. Take the long look. We plan, we study, and we prepare for everything in life that is worthwhile. There are no foolproof formulas for successful marriages but if we look at ours at long range and live it day by day, we can be happy. There are some tracking stations and some signals along the way. There are human tools we can use. Use them! Settle down for the long haul and make your marriage a happy one.

7 *Children Are for Happiness*

To want children is as natural for you as the desire to have a life companion. It is the supreme manifestation of your growth as a person. When a couple is ready for this important step, the experience of parenthood is supremely fulfilling. The forces that lead us to become parents are strong. There has never been found a substitute for the satisfactions that come from bringing children into the world and rearing them.

For a woman, being a parent brings great satisfaction and a unique fulfillment. The bearing and rearing of children is, beyond question, a female's greatest achievement and the climax of her erotic expression. It is not only her greatest joy, but the source of her greatest power. As an old cliché states, "No home is complete without a family."

Let us remember, however, a truth we are in danger of forgetting, that fathers are parents too. Although some men seem at times to be indifferent or even hostile to the idea of having children, yet deep in their hearts they, too, find the height of joy in becoming a "papa." One father expressed it with open honesty.

> My day-old son is plenty scrawny,
> His mouth is wide with screams, or yawny,
> His ears seem larger than he's needing,
> His nose is flat, his chin's receding,
> His skin is very, very red,
> He has no hair upon his head,

> And yet I'm proud as proud can be
> To hear you say he looks like me.

Surely no couple, unless there are some strong reasons for it, would ever enter marriage with the deliberate intention of permanently avoiding parenthood. Unquestionably, there can be no exaltation of spirit quite like that which comes when you see your newborn son or daughter before your eyes. One who has experienced it can never forget the moment when the little face wrinkles up for the first breath of life and the cry that tells you *your* child is born into the world. Nothing can equal it.

One of the most significant contributions that a couple will make to the world is to be healthy and righteous parents. Not only, however, is this our duty—it is our highest privilege and brings the greatest joy. Those who know the delights of children cannot comprehend a deliberately childless home, where the door never slams and the cry of "mother" never echoes up the stairway. Fathers also share in this joy. It is an inheritance that has come down from the beginning of time. God gives us the privilege of being like him in many ways. There is no higher sense in which we share in the image of God than in the ability to create life through the processes that he has ordained.

How Soon and How Many?

There are, of course, no hard-and-fast answers for these two matters. Conditions vary and people are different. In order to evaluate the matter objectively, some questions have been raised by students in the field. Since they are helpful in considering these two important decisions, every couple which is weighing the matter of parenthood should consider them carefully.

1. If the first child is delayed, is it not possible that the couple will be enabled to give their children a better start in life?
2. What will one, two, or more offspring do to a family's mode of living, to its probable future, to the advancement

of the parents and the education of the children?

3. For how long and to what extent will motherhood withdraw an employed wife from income-producing employment?

4. What price in personal welfare will the other members of the family have to pay for each additional child?

5. What is likely to happen to a wife's health if her children are not spaced out enough to permit adequate recovery after each birth?

6. What are the social, intellectual, and emotional consequences of a child's membership in a large or small family?

In considering these questions, a couple should remember that although it is important to be financially able to bring a child into the world, at the same time one can wait too long and insist on too much financial security. Most parents, in looking back at the early years, realize that their character has been strengthened by the sacrifices that they have been called upon to make in order to provide for their children. This truth should be underscored: *It is unwise to wait too long, though there should be time for adjustments and for necessary savings.*

A couple should not forget the age factor. The experts disagree on exactly the best age for a woman to have a baby, but it is certainly true that as one gets into the middle and late twenties for the first child they are approaching a time which is not as good as the earlier years for beginning the family. Also, a couple should remember that they do not want to be too old to enjoy their children during the high school and even college years. Although to give definite and specific advice is always dangerous, it does seem that it is best to have the children within a year or two after marriage unless the marriage has been an unusually early one or an unusually late one.

The number of children a couple should have will also vary. During the 1920's, college graduates regarded more than one or two children as "unfashionable, careless, or ostentatious." During the 1960's, however, the average college student thought in terms of three or four children. In fact, a poll during those years showed that on a national basis marriageable young people considered the ideal number of children in the following way: 2 percent thought the ideal family was no children; 42 percent, one or two children; 48 percent, three or four children; and 8 percent, five or more children.

During the 1970's it is becoming increasingly more expensive to rear children. Years ago, on the farm, they were an economic asset. A kid could always earn his keep. Today, any way you look at it, in most families they are an economic liability. An outstanding life insurance company made a study of the cost of rearing children a few years ago. It varies, of course, according to the salary of the family and the standard of living. At that time, the study showed that the total cost of rearing a child up to eighteen years of age in families with an income of $5,000 to $10,000 per year will average $20,785. This does not include the cost of public education and other services furnished by the community. Nor does it take into consideration the value of the personal services which are furnished by the mother. Each family will make its own decision. Even then plans go astray and unwanted children come. Certainly it does not need to be said that a family should never allow the "unplanned-for-child" to suffer emotionally by wrong attitudes on the part of the parents. Children are expensive but most parents would say they are worth every bit of the sacrifice and struggle.

Adjustments Are Necessary

Bringing children into the world means a considerable dislocation of the routines of married life. It is a stern test of a marriage.

The great problem when children arrive is to keep our zest and pleasure as we seek to be good parents and yet remain responsible and watchful. One thing needs to remain constantly before us—life, either with children or without them, is unlikely to offer perfect solutions to problems. Life with children is not too different from married life. Both are carried on in a perpetual state of unstable equilibrium, held upright by the belief that something hopefully satisfactory lies just around the corner. Of course, there will be some genuinely black days and some permanent disappointments. On the other hand, there will also be many hours each day that make us sure the "game is worth the candle."

A man must adjust to the fact that his wife is now a mother also. This means several things. First, it means that she will be tired more often—and more tired than ever before. This will mean, frankly, that there will be more times when she is not in the mood for lovemaking. This does not mean that she has become frigid. This does not mean that she is mistreating him. It merely means that she is physically exhausted.

A man must accept something else. The wife does not love him less because she devotes time to the child or children. He must be mature enough not to become jealous of her affection for the child. The household will begin to revolve around the baby and the man must adjust to this without resenting the situation. New responsibilities have come, and there must be adjustment to the new routine.

It may be that for a few months, at least, the father will begin to wonder whether the pleasures of having a family outweigh the hardships. Most men simply do not respond to a young baby with the fascination and absorption of most women who can be interested in the very small details of tending to the baby. The average man will probably often think that his home has suddenly been changed into a woman's world where he counts for little or nothing. Man must adjust. He must not allow his pride to cause him to act in an immature way.

For the woman, also, there are adjustments. For one thing, she must remember that although she has become a mother she is still a wife. She still has obligations to her husband. Many a man who has never had an affair with a woman becomes unfaithful first during the period of his wife's pregnancy or during those months after the baby comes home when he feels that his wife has lost interest in him as a person. This does

not mean the man is justified. Sexual immorality and unfaithfulness are wrong whatever the extenuating circumstances. But the
wise woman will continue to save some of her physical strength
and kind words for her husband. If she does not, she may end
up being sorry!

Another adjustment a woman must make is to realize that,
whether it is fair or not, she is going to bear most of the brunt
of housework and adjustments as the children develop. Regardless of whether it is right or not, this tongue-in-cheek picture
is realistic,

> Father has sick leave
>   Mother has us
> When father is sick,
>   He makes a fuss.
>
> He takes to his bed
>   And takes a large pill
> Mother, of course,
>   Never is ill.

In most situations the man lets the woman assume all the
responsibilities. She will probably be the first one up each morning and apt to be the last one to bed at night. The kitchen,
bedroom, living room, bathroom, and den are all her provinces.
There are some men who are helpful at some times, but generally
mother will be the one to do most, if not all, of the housework.
Husband and children alike, far too often, take mother for
granted. This is not fair. It is grossly unfair! But it is a reality!
The "getting-ready rhyme" is an actuality in most homes,

> Sing a song of swivets!
>   Papa's in the shower.
> He'll hog the steamy sanctum
>   At least another hour.
>
> Baby's dressed and waiting
>   And what on earth's she doing,

So quiet in the kitchen?
Opening the blueing.

Junior's in the basement
Accumulating dirt,
And sister's in the bedroom
Wailing, fix her skirt!

And guess who's in a tizzy
And steady, woman, steady,
When set to go, they chorus,
"Gee, Mom, aren't you ready!"

Mother, the children are yours! It is true they are father's also but you had better be prepared to face the fact that most men are reluctant when it comes to doing household chores and accepting the full responsibilities of parenthood. Someone has said very aptly, "Fatherhood is imposed upon a man without inquiring whether or not he is equal to the task. That is why there are so many fathers who have children, but so few children who have fathers." Whether or not you like it, and whether or not it is fair, mother, the major adjustment will be with you.

But They Are Worth It

Of course, children are problems! It is difficult to discipline them. One frustrated parent wrote

Our children never mind the snow
The rain or chilly weather;
Exposed to all the blasts that blow,
They play outdoors together.

They never mind the chilblained skin
As they enjoy their breather,
And when we call them sharply in
They never mind us either.

They do not know the meaning of "staying clean." A modern mother complained,

If, via streamlined stratosphere,
My son could travel far
Vacation on the milky way
Commute from star to star.

Even as he winged his way,
With speed of light through outer space,
Large portions of his well loved earth,
Would darken elbows, ears and face.

But this is not an insuperable problem. Another modern mother rejoices as she says,

Oh, if there's a coal bin,
The small fry will crawl in it.
If there's a puddle,
Be sure they will sprawl in it.
Blithely intent on
Consuming their pounds of dirt,
Life for the moppets
Is one giddy round of dirt.
Squirting what's squirtable,
Squashing what's squashable,
Children, thank Heaven,
Are guaranteed washable!

They, expecially the boys, are sloppy around the house. A perplexed mother complains,

My son is expert every fall
At picking up a fumbled ball
A ball not easily pickable
Therefore it is inexplicable
And difficult to understand
Why any boy so deft of hand
In football's fierce and frantic throws
At home cannot pick up his clothes.

Girls are likewise unmanageable and unpredictable. Listen to some profound advice on "How to Handle a Teenage Daughter":

Ask her to do the dinner dishes
(She'll do her homework)
Tell her to clean the room
(She'll set her hair)
Rave about her latest steady
(She'll start dating ten other boys)
Comment favorably on her eye makeup
(She'll cut down on the lid liner)
Admire the way she's wearing her hair
(She won't put it up on rollers twice a day)
Tell her she looks better plump than skinny
(She'll stop eating ice cream for breakfast)
Ask her to set her hair
(She'll clean her room)
Tell her to do her homework
(She'll do the dinner dishes)

Yes, they are worth it! They can cause us irritation, yet satisfaction; grief, yet joy; embarrassment, yet genuine delight. A girl can muss up our home, our hair, and our dignity. She can spend our money, waste our time, and spoil our temper. But just about the time our patience is exhausted and we are about to go to pieces, her sunshine floods our soul and we know she's worth it. As Alan Beck said, "A girl is a nerve-racking nuisance . . . a noisy bundle of mischief. But when your dreams tumble down and the world is in a mess—when it seems you are pretty much of a fool after all—she can make you a king when she climbs on your knee and whispers, 'I love you best of all!' "

Likewise a boy is the same. You may lock him out of your workshop but you can't lock him out of your heart. You might push him out of your study but he is still in your mind. As Alan Beck also said, "Might as well give up—he is your captor, your jailer, your boss, and your master—a freckle-faced, pint-sized, cat-chasing bundle of noise. But when you come home at night with only the shattered pieces of your hopes and dreams, he can mend them like new with the two magic words—'Hi,

Dad!' " Never forget that they are worth every bit of trouble, every bit of expense! Children are for happiness!

Some Important Suggestions

A recent writer was discussing the flurry of new books on child care that had been published that month. She said, "They cover such a wide range of theory and practice that in them you can find any 'expert' support for almost any stand you want to take with your small fry." There is no end to the amount of advice that is being given. At the risk of joining the ranks and being another of this inglorious group we are listing several specific suggestions concerning children:

1. *Imbue them with ideals.* If "imitation is the sincerest form of flattery," then the ability to make a person want to imitate you is the highest form of teaching. Don't preach to your children. Give them an example. More than that, however, create within them a thirst for high standards of living as you encourage their resourcefulness and creativity. A Catholic minister, with an unusually successful record of dealing with children, tells of a teenage boy who has had remarkable success in painting. Although he has never had professional training, he has received a number of awards for his work. This young man credits a junior high teacher with developing his interest in art. He says that she loaned him some paints and gave him some paints and gave him a piece of canvass. He continues, "She was the best teacher I ever had, not only for developing my interest in art, but for opening up a lot of new doors. She was the greatest." The minister says, "The efforts of teachers, parents, and religious leaders to imbue young people with high ideals do pay off . . . cooperate with the Lord by making the most of the opportunities he provides to inspire boys and girls." Such an attitude is biblical. The writer of Hebrews says, "Let us consider and give attention, continuous care to . . . studying how we may stir up (stim-

ulate and incite) to love and helpful deeds and noble activities" (Heb. 10:24, Amplified).

2. *Accept their limitations—and yours.* When a baby is on the way toward birth, the parents cannot help but dream. They project far into the future and idealize what their child will be like. Perhaps he will be a boy with strong scientific interests—a real leader. Or, if the baby is a girl, she will be a wonderful companion for them and someday marry a successful man. This dream child is a very important person and does help to ease the transition to the real child who will probably be entirely different. The day comes, of course, when we have to give up the dream and get acquainted with the actual child. It isn't easy to accept limitations in the people that you love dearly. But we must do it. Sometimes we even have to face the acceptance of a child who has physical deficiencies or even severe mental retardation. Dr. W. A. Criswell once told, at a pastors' conference, of how he gave to a mother, who had learned of her child's retardation, a beautiful concept of life. He said, "Young lady, the Lord had a child coming into the world that was not going to be right. He looked all over the world to find a man and woman who would know how to give love and guidance to the child. He chose you and your husband for this high honor. Now he wants you to take care of this child and give it the affection and help that it needs." Some may feel this is a naive concept of God and faith, but many people have found that such faith helps them to accept the limitations of their children. It is no reflection on a parent that a child has shortcomings in certain areas. Learn to live with these limitations. You will be happy and, you will be able to lead your child into a well-adjusted and useful life.

3. *Build emotional health in your child.* How do you do it? The best way is for husband and wife to have a love relationship with each other that will provide a stable and

affectionate atmosphere in the home. This, as perhaps no other one thing, will foster healthy attitudes and adjustments in the children. If a real love exists between parents, there is scarcely any likelihood of one parent seeking exclusive possession of the child. Where the husband-wife relationship is faulty, and parents use the child to fulfill their own ungratified longings, the home becomes a breeding ground for many undesirable qualities in the child. If a woman is unhappy in her marriage, she may single out her son as a husband substitute. The father may do the same with a daughter. A psychiatrist with keen insight tells us that very young children frequently become showcases for the personal maladjustments of their parents. While it is important for a parent to love a child, it is even more important for a child to know that mother and daddy love each other than for him to know that they love him. Even when the child is very tiny, he can sense emotional disturbances which are usually channeled through the mother in the form of anxieties. It cannot be emphasized too strongly that parents need to love each other if they would produce children who are free of fears and immaturities.

4. *Do not minimize discipline.* Within recent years we have seen the pendulum swing among the child-guidance experts from the old attitude of severe discipline all the way to permissiveness with little, if any, discipline. Wise thinkers are now on the way back. We are being told now that children want discipline. Even when they seem to be rebelling against it, they are inwardly crying out for it. The child should be disciplined with firmness and reason. We should not make threats in anger nor should we make impossible promises. Too often, parents are afraid that if they discipline the child he will come to hate them. For that reason one parent will seek to let the other parent do the "dirty work." One famous columnist says, "Discipline your child—don't let your anger throw you off balance. If he knows you

are fair, you will not lose his respect or his love." Extreme
freedom for the child has been weighed and found wanting!
One teacher speaks wisely:

> I must not interfere with any child, I have been told
> To bend his will to mine, or try to shape him through
>   some mold
> Of thought. Naturally, as a flower he must unfold.
> Yet flowers have the discipline of wind and rain,
> And though I know it gives the gardener much pain,
> I have seen him use his pruning shears to gain
> More strength and beauty for some blossoms bright.
> And he would do whatever he thought right
> To save his flowers from a deadening blight.
> I do not know—yet it does seem to me
> That only *weeds* unfold just naturally.

Let us remember that love is the basis of all our dealing
with our children. It is neither silly sweetness nor weak
sentimentality, but a deep, strong selfless devotion. Such
a love enables us to say no firmly and mean it. Do you
want your child to be a flower or a weed?

5. *Recognize their individualities.* Perhaps the cruelest thing
a parent or teacher can do is to compare brothers or sisters.
Here, for instance, is an older boy who is a brilliant student.
Everything he does in school seems to be right. His younger
brother may have just as many abilities, but grade-making
is not one of them. To compare these children is cruel.
It accomplishes nothing except increasing hostilities. Some
children become so completely crushed by comparisons that
they give up completely and refuse to do anything. In this
way they cannot suffer from being compared. Often the
casual, seemingly sloppy, good-natured boy will go further
in life and be more successful than the brainy kid who
makes "straight A's" and wins all the awards. Let each
child be himself. Don't force him into the mold of another.

6. *Prepare them for life's disillusionments.* Someday your children must leave the nest. They must face a world that is frustrating and sometimes even hostile. How do you get them ready? It isn't easy to know how. Someone told jokingly of a new puzzle for children that prepares them for coping with today's world. The puzzle is so designed that any way the child puts it together it's wrong.

Of course, we should never crush our children's spirits by forcing problems upon them that are too difficult for their abilities, but they should be allowed to meet face to face the disappointments and conflicts of normal experience. Pain, tension, and disillusionment are a part of life.

> The world will never adjust itself
> To suit your whims to the letter
> Some things will go wrong
> Your whole life long
> And the sooner you know it the better.

Neither are we suggesting that a parent should promiscuously expose children to all of the sins and vices of our contemporary way of life with the flippant remark, "He's got to see the evil of the world sometime. I'll take him to all of the sophisticated places of amusement early and show him what life in the raw really is." This is extreme and can be a dangerous approach to life.

Somewhere between the extreme of overprotectionism and overexposure is a happy middle-of-the-road attitude. Your child is an individual. One of the finest things you will ever teach him is to accept responsibility. Let us never forget that the oversolicitous parent who feels he's "protecting" his children actually is crippling them. Overprotection prevents children from developing their own methods of dealing with the inevitable unpleasant experiences and puts youngsters at a great disadvantage. Let them face life in their own strength but with the certainty that you are nearby to help them if they get into serious trouble. Teach them to make their own decisions, but this does not mean give them absolute freedom without any discipline. It's not easy but the wise parent will help them understand something of the rugged world outside even while they are surrounded with the security of love in a beautiful home environment.

Enjoy Them Now

One thing we need to remember! Our children will be gone from us sooner than we realize! Clarence Darrow is reported to have said once, in a cynical moment, "The first half of our lives is ruined by our parents and the second half by our children." Our years as parents of growing children, however, will not be ruined if we will try to enjoy them while they are still with us.

Of course, they are a lot of trouble! They bother us, irritate us, and cause us many sleepless hours of anxiety and worry. They scheme and plot how they can wrap us around their thumbs. One experienced parent says:

> The years when children can be trained
> Are futilely too few;
> Before the goal can be attained
> They've started training you!

But the years fly quickly! A father once said to his son what many fathers have said, "I'll be so glad when you grow up!" He meant that he would be glad when the child quit acting in an irresponsible manner and assumed maturity. All of us have these periods. But the mother said later to her husband, "Please don't ever say that again. That's the trouble—they'll be grown up before we realize it."

This does not mean that we should ignore their immaturities and overlook their inconsistencies. We must teach them responsibility. This is one of our greatest tasks. But one of the greatest privileges we have is to enjoy them and let them be children while they are children. One counselor in the field says, "Children are not small adults. They do not think, feel, or react as adults do. They do not have the knowledge, judgment, or background to choose experiences that will be beneficial to them and reject those that may be harmful . . . we cannot judge or measure them by adult standards." Enjoy your children and let them be children!

> They'll not be with us very long
> Enjoy them while you can.
> That girl will soon a woman be
> That boy, likewise, a man.
>
> They'll not be with us very long
> But they are yours today.
> The time is short, enjoy those kids
> Before they move away.

Children are for happiness. The psalmist says they are a "gift of the Eternal." He compares children to "arrows in an archer's hand" and concludes, "Happy the man who has a quiver full of them" (Ps. 127:3-4, Moffatt).

8 The Harvest Years

All of us shrink from the phenomenon of "getting old." One fellow, however, wisely said, "It's not too bad though when you consider the alternative." Many of us smile sympathetically with one man's "Advice to Be Ignored."

> If time is rushing by—in truth
> That's what we taught it in our youth
>
> How we did urge acceleration:
> Hurry, Christmas! Come vacation!
>
> Impatiently we waited for
> The gifts that slow time held in store.
>
> Now other youngsters in our place
> Coax it to move with swifter pace.
>
> Dear boys and girls, don't try to speed it,
> For oh, so soon, you're going to need it!

"Youth is a glorious time of life," said one, "it's a shame to waste it on young people." About the time we begin to mature sufficiently to handle some of our family problems we find they are gone—not merely our problems, but *our families* are gone!

A Definition of Terms

What are the harvest years? In attempting to arrive at a workable definition, the writer asked a number of people this question. The responses were many and varied. The usual answer is "the time of retirement—the golden years of life." There is, of course, some truth in this evaluation.

Is there not, however, more to it? Do not these years begin sometimes even before the children leave home? If we accept Webster's secondary definition of "harvest" as "to win by achievement," the following lady was already in her harvest years:

> In stores, on streets, in church, at tea,
> The high school girls all speak to me.
> I'm greeted with a bright "hello"
> From those I do not even know.
> Some other mothers are ignored
> Not me, I'm practically adored,
> What makes me such a reigning queen?
> I have a handsome son, eighteen.

Shortly after World War II, Janet Baird published an edited volume entitled *The Harvest Years*. It carried as a subtitle "A Guide to Abundant Living After Forty." Perhaps we are safe in saying this period begins about the time the children begin to become responsible citizens and extends down to the time of retirement and beyond.

The Empty Nest

Sylvia Porter recently put her first child on the plane for college. It prompted her to devote one of her columns to this, what she called, "phenomenon of modern times." She pointed out some interesting and provocative truths. For instance, fifty years ago the average American family knew little of an empty nest. If one developed, it was shortly terminated. One of the two parents would die. But things have changed now! We have earlier marriages, smaller families, and longer life spans. Although the empty nest period now averages fourteen years, some couples will live together for thirty or forty years from the time their last child leaves home until one of the two passes away.

Everything about this period is by no means bad! There are some real virtues! For one thing, the beginning of it is often the most affluent of all periods. The husband is at the peak of his earning years. It can easily be the least debt-burdened period. True, education debts may plague the first part, but these can be paid and the couple can be financially free as never before. By this time, most couples will own their own home. Many women in their forties will go back to work or continue working. This can give added income to prepare for the final years. If, as you read these words, you are still a young mother, keep your education and your training up to date. Study at home and, if possible, take refresher courses. Be ready in case you need, either emotionally or financially, to go to work either part time or full time.

There are, however, some emotional problems connected with the empty nest. The most obvious is that of being lonesome for the children. A wise person will begin early to prepare for the permanent separation. One couple, seeing the final severance coming, allowed the last child to be gone for extended periods of time during the remaining two or three years before he left for college. He worked away from home one summer. He took several trips during holiday seasons. This helped to prepare for the day when he would be gone completely.

A husband and wife will face another serious problem. They will be back with each other exclusively as in the early years of marriage. If they have grown apart during the years of rearing their family, it will be immediately evident.

Perhaps the most serious emotional problem, however, is that you probably now consider yourself in the last general period of your life. There will be sub-periods within this area, but it is easy to grow disturbed as one faces this final division of life's span.

Become Reacquainted

The basic purpose for marriage does not vary. It is the same for all periods of a man and woman's life. Part of many wedding rituals is that a man and woman should cleave unto each other. The expression is often used "until death do us part." We should remember that, although this includes the early days of marriage with all of its adjustments and the busy days when the small children crowd the house, it also includes the years when children leave and loneliness and uncertainty invade the hearts of the married couple.

Life does not stop because the children have gone. There is much more to it, and you are now standing upon the threshold of what can be your best years. Your marriage should now be more meaningful than ever before. Theodore F. Adams says, "Mature love can be even finer and sweeter than youthful romantic love. It can grow in depth and understanding. When you are young your lives touch at a few very important points, but as you grow older life touches at every point." Much of the beauty of young love is retained, but there is added to it a depth because of your mutual understanding of each other. There will be a greater tenderness and sympathy during these days of renewed affection. Did you ever attempt a second honeymoon while you were still in the early years of your marriage? Many have and found that it did not work out. There were too many distractions and anxieties about matters at home. It was impossible to relax when the mind was on children, budgets, and other household problems. One couple, with problems still at home, did not fare so well on their premature attempt at a second honeymoon. He wrote about it,

> They scramble the trail to Lookout Point
> And watch as the dawn unfurls,
> Alone, these two, with the fabulous view.
> And the first words are the girl's:
>   "George, I don't see why you keep saying we
>   can't afford
>   color TV. My goodness, if we can afford a
>   trip like this—"

The falls are majestic and old as time.
There are rainbows in the spray.
And she stands at his side like a pensive bride.
And what does the darling say?
  "George, I have the most horrible feeling I
  went off and left
  the water running in the washbowl. The
  phone rang and—"

But now it's night, and the mountaintops
Finger the stars above.
And she turns her eyes from the glittering skies
And speaks to her legal love:
  "George, do you think I ought to take those
  rhinestones off
  of my blue chiffon? They look sort of outré."

In the "harvest years," however, you are in a position to take a completely enjoyable honeymoon. You should be able to do it without any problems or worries about matters at home. You may be surprised at the depth of the experience. Although the passions of youth have faded away, many older couples testify that even the physical aspects of marriage are more richly and deeply satisfying in these harvest years. Adjustments have been made, and needs are more easily met because of years together. The complete relaxation and freedom from both drudgeries and anxieties produce a true oneness in contemplation, expectation, and realization.

Keep Your Flexibility

A prominent medical doctor tells us that a man usually reacts to his fortieth birthday in one of two ways, "It may hit him as crushing and undeniable proof that he is getting old and will soon be on the shelf, or he may find, with considerable surprise, that being forty is not so very different except that he seems to have a little more sense and judgment and a clearer idea of the goals toward which he is working." Age is a state of mind—not a measurement on the calendar. No person needs to grow old in spirit. There is too much around to challenge us and keep our minds active and growing.

One of the common expressions to designate aging people is that they are "set in their ways." A more dignified way of stating this would be they are "resistant to change." This is another way of saying they have lost their flexibility. It is when our minds are no longer limber—when we have lost our flexibility—that old age is upon us!

There are, of course, medical reasons for deterioration of the mind—such things as brain damage from strokes or injuries. The best medical opinions, however, assure us that most personality changes are unrelated to this type of problem. The brain of the senile person appears, under examination, no different from the brain of the normal aged person. Even the most agile mind tends to grow old. An outstanding neuro-surgeon points out that the more authoritative a person has been in earlier years, the more marked are the compensating reactions producing inferiority and inadequacy as he grows older. He illustrates, "The loss of being the central figure in the family, the mother or the father, is often keenly felt and may be accompanied by a mild depression caused by a sense of loneliness or isolation." A man who was rigid in his thinking in earlier years will tend to become even more restricted as he reaches the middle and later years.

Keep the mind growing! All of the "experts" agree that the soundness of your body depends in considerable measure upon the soundness of your mental outlook. There is no doubt but that a disturbed, unhappy mind is a great ally of physical deterioration and decay. On the other hand, nothing makes for a healthy mind more than constant freshness because of flexibility and growth. We do not have to become introspective, moody, peevish, and melancholy in the middle years and later. We can keep the sunny and cheerful disposition of youth if we will keep our minds flexible—always responding to new situations. Let's be honest about it! The solution to our mental and emotional needs lies to a great extent in our own hands.

All of these facts are related to our marriage. Too much is at stake for us to ignore them. Boredom can make a marriage go sour. Living in a small, narrow, circumscribed world can squeeze the lifeblood from wedded happiness. The flexible mind means the well rounded life. The type of person who fits this pattern is one who respects himself without conceit, who has been guided by principles but who has refrained from being a slave to dogma, who has steadiness of purpose but has resisted the temptation to become hypnotized by an immutable goal, who has bent his energies to making the grade rather than getting to the top first, who has faced honestly and tolerated his weaknesses while employing his strengths, who has respected his neighbors but has also maintained pride in himself. If the "mind is the measure of the man," we need to keep it flexible and thus assure its creativity.

Being Grandparents

This period of life brings a great thrill—you are now ready to be grandparents. Can anything be more wonderful? One new grandparent commented on the joy of her new role, "What I like is I can hold the baby till he cries and then give him back to his mother." One of the strange phenomena of this time is that you reevaluate people. For instance, isn't it a bit ludicrous that the boy who two years ago was a childish, immature lad not nearly good enough for your daughter has suddenly become capable of being the father of the most intelligent and best-looking child in the community?

There is a vast difference in being grandparents now and several generations ago. It hasn't been too long since the common pattern was "three generations under one roof" in a large farmhouse. Later the son and wife would build a home down the road a few hundred feet but still help dad work the land. The urban situation has changed this greatly. Longevity at one end and early marriages at the other has introduced a new situation. The "five layer cake" is now sociological terminology. By this we mean that along with the split-level ranch house and the two-car garage, America now has the "five generation family." Think of it! A forty-five-year-old person can face the dual role and responsibility of being both a grandparent and a grandchild. Did you know that there are hundreds of thousands of such families in America today? There are certain serious implications in such a growing condition, but isn't it a thrilling prospect for you to think that there is a good chance *you* might live to see your great-great grandchild. This is a distinct possibility!

What happier harvest could you want for your maturing years? You've just begun to live! As Al Jolson used to say, "You ain't seen nothing yet!"

Particular Problems of Middle Age

Of course, everything will not be perfect. As in every stage of life, you will need to make adjustments. Mothers, perhaps more than fathers, will miss being needed by the children. At first, you may jokingly say that it is a "good miss" but this is not the whole picture. It can be a shock to find out that no one is depending upon you. Part of life's fulfillment is in making a definite contribution to meeting the needs of others. You may now find an outlet through church and community service. There are many fine civic and social work agencies that need the contribution which mature people are able to make. Gaines S. Dobbins urges middle-age parents not to drop out of either church or community activities. He contends that they need both the fellowship and stimulation of jobs. Furthermore, they need to keep thinking and to be challenged by worthwhile tasks which need to be done. This period can be the most fruitful period of service in one's life.

Another problem concerns the relationship we should sustain with our married children. Certainly we do not want to interfere. On the other hand, even married children need their parents.

Now it is in a different way. Young married couples are able to appreciate their parents as never before. As they face the problems of marriage's early years, it will have a great stabilizing effect on them if they can see their parents adjusting to the middle years and living happily together. It will give them new courage to face their problems and strong confidence in the institution of marriage.

Perhaps one of the greatest problems is when we find the world is making its pitch to another group of people—a younger set. For example, *Redbook Magazine,* several years ago, ran a campaign based on the slogan "Some Girls Are Too Old for *Redbook.* 18 to 34: These are the *Redbook* Years." These advertisements consisted of a series of cartoons showing a young attractive lady and a rather unattractive dumpy woman (the latter was about thirty-five years of age). In one advertisement the younger one was buying expensive goodies while the other one had a hot water bottle. In another, the young girl was buying sweet-smelling items while the thirty-five-year-old had only one unscented bar of soap. Think of the effect of such advertisements on a forty-three-year-old woman! A man faces a similar problem. The exercise charts list ages for different instructions. Imagine his feeling when he finds his age down at the very bottom or even omitted because he's too old for this type of exercise!

What is the solution for the depression caused by such experiences? The yardstick is to decide what is your lifetime goal. Keen observers of modern trends point out that every society has some sort of "carrot" to dangle before you as a lifetime goal. In our society it is probably the middle aged period when this "carrot" can mean the most to us. There was a recent study made by Viennese psychologists who divided striving into five stages. With a slight revision, they fit competitive American society today. Consider these:

(1) Exploratory stage—between the ages about fifteen and twenty-seven, when we finish school and are trying to decide on our lifetime goal

(2) Selective maturity—between about twenty-eight and forty-two, when we decide on our goal and put all our efforts into trying to achieve it

(3) Testing stage—beginning at about forty-three, when we start to reflect on our lives to determine whether we have achieved our goal and to wonder if things have turned out as we planned

(4) Indulgent stage—beginning at about forty-eight when we try to concentrate on getting the maximum satisfaction and gratification out of the "prime of life"

(5) Completion—from about sixty-five, when we look back on life and begin to live in the past and usually stop seeking a further goal

In order to weather the depression of middle age, we must quit thinking in terms of age and think in terms of goals. We are now in a position to reap the fruit of the hard work of other years. We are now mature enough to remove ourselves from the competitive role that society forces upon us. We now have sufficient judgment to realize that inward contentment is the goal of life, not mere status or image. In the immature years we adopt the premise that a person is considered successful according to the standards that society sets up. As we become emotionally mature, we decide that the competitive game is simply not worth the struggle. If we are happily adjusted with our companion, we can be literally "sitting on top of the world." Merely because we have passed one stage in life does not mean that we are about to go to the grave or become permanently disabled. Actually, we are now in the most glorious era of life. We are past the immaturities and superficialities of youth, but we still have many more years left in which to enjoy the worthwhile things of abundant living.

Live Life Out

Of course, the "golden years" will eventually come. This is inevitable, but even these days can be happy ones. One college

president spent thirty years as a successful teacher and adminis-
trator. After retiring, he still kept busy in what he called "my
own graduate school." He said, "The important thing is to *live
life out.* Suppose the trees decided to give up the ghost early
in the summer? Suppose they just gave up and decided to drop
all their leaves during the summertime? Consider all the beautiful
time of green and growing they would miss out on. And look
at all the pleasure of which they'd deprive the rest of us!" He
and his wife practiced this philosophy in their personal lives.
They had a marvelous companionship until the very end. He
testified, "My wife and I both think our old age has been pretty
wonderful—but it didn't just happen that way. In order to keep
young, we've cultivated new ideas, learned about new things.
In order to stay really alive, we've kept drinking from the waters
of life; we have surrounded ourselves with life; we are *living
life out.*"

It is impossible to overemphasize the importance of keeping
both one's independence and individuality during the "golden
years." One of the saddest sights to be seen is one who has
become sorry for himself. Part of maintaining individual identity
and integrity is financial security. Long before the golden years
come, plans for a retirement program can be begun. In some
business situations, gradual retirement is encouraged. This prevents one from waking up suddenly to the fact he is "on the
shelf." Above all, do not allow yourself as an individual or as
a couple to be completely dependent on others, either financially
or emotionally. In fact, let the opposite be true! Learn to help
others! There are literally hundreds of ways to "keep alive all
your life." One of the most important is to become a "friendly
visitor." Make it your job to visit at least one ill or needy person
every day. Your own life will be brightened as you bring happiness into theirs.

Looking hopefully to the future always gives added meaning
to life. In fact, in *Grow Lovely Growing Old,* Mrs. Douglas
Scarbrough McDaniel puts it strongly. She says, "Old age begins

. . . the very day one ceases to impinge hopefully on the future."
Hope is the last thing that dies in man. It conducts us in an
easier and more pleasant way to our journey's end. Rochefou-
cauld says, "Hope . . . serves to carry us to the end of life by
a pleasant road." Shelley agrees and adds a new dimension,

> But hope will make thee young for Hope
> and Youth
> Are children of one mother, even love.

Live life out—creatively and hopefully! A person grows old with
the hardening of the ideas, not the arteries.

Stay in Love

A marriage can last and be beautiful down to the very end
of life. Almost every day you can read in the paper of a couple
celebrating fifty years of life together. Many of these husbands
and wives remain in love and are continuously interested in
the other's welfare. These couples will never grow old to each
other. They will continue to show mutual devotion and affection.
But it is not easy. A permanent marriage must be more than
a merely erotic union based on physical relationships. This is
especially true after sixty. The ideal marriage has to be one
of many interests besides the one of sex. If sex is still of interest
to older persons, all well and good, but the main objective in
later years is that there be a blending of feelings, a coalescing
of interests, in short a true love partnership. By the time you
have come to these years there should be a perfect adjustment
and blending of personalities. There should be a respect for
the desires of the other which will aid greatly in attaining a
lasting love and understanding. There should be complete compatibility in order that the closing years of life shall be the
happiest.

Of course, one partner will, in all probability, go before the
other. Do you remember a beautiful story from one of the
childhood readers? An elderly couple had performed a deed

of kindness for a stranger. The stranger turned out to be an angel and told the couple that he would grant them any one wish they desired. Do you know what they wanted? They asked that neither one would outlive the other. In the story the angel turned both of them to giant oak trees and for many years they dwelt side by side in the field near their house. In practical living, however, we must inevitably face separation.

What about the world to come? Certainly the relationships will be spiritual rather than physical. Our Master said, "In the resurrection they neither marry nor are given in marriage" (Matt. 22:30). Will we know each other as husband and wife in heaven? Not in the physical sense. But, since relationships in heaven are spiritual, it seems that a husband and wife who have lived together and become a part of each other's life should certainly be closer in spirit to each other than to any other person in heaven. Perhaps this is what Elizabeth Barrett Browning was speaking about in her beautiful sonnet,

> How do I love thee? Let me count the ways.
> I love thee to the depth and breadth and height
> My soul can reach. . . .
>
> . . . .
>
> I love thee with a love I seemed to lose
> With my lost saints. I love thee with the breath,
> Smiles, tears, of all my life!—and, if God choose,
> I shall but love thee better after death.

There are a few beautiful stories of couples passing away in separate rooms at almost exactly the same time. In this way one is not required to outlive the other. Most marriages, however, witness the passing of one and the leaving of another here. Of course, many times the one left marries again. This is certainly understandable and to be encouraged when such a one can find a companion for the lonely years. Yet, it is beautiful to see two come down the years together united in spirit and with a comradeship growing more blessed as the days go by. One couple did this and when the first passed away the second wrote:

> Should you go first and I remain
> To walk the road alone,
> I'll live in memory's garden, dear,
> With happy days we've known.
> In Spring I'll wait for roses red
> When fade the lilac's blue,
> In early Fall when brown leaves call
> I'll catch a glimpse of you.
>
> Should you go first and I remain
> For battles to be fought,
> Each thing you've touched along the way
> Will be a hallowed spot.
> I'll hear your voice, I'll see your smile,
> Though blindly I may grope,
> The memory of your helping hand
> Will buoy me on with hope.
>
> Should you go first and I remain
> To finish with the scroll,
> No lengthening shadows shall creep in
> To make this life seem droll.
> We've known so much of happiness,
> We've had our cup of joy,
> And memory is one gift of God
> That death cannot destroy.
>
> Should you go first and I remain,
> One thing I'd have you do;
> Walk slowly down the path of death,
> For soon I'll follow you.
> I want to know each step you take
> That I may walk the same,
> For someday down that lonely road
> You'll hear me call your name.

There is nothing in the Bible that disputes the fact we can "love each other better after death."

9 *Religion and the Home*

In his definitive work *The Changing American Family,* Roger Crook reminds us that the more a couple have in common, both in background and in interests, the better are their prospects for success in marriage. He says, "Most studies of marital success have discovered a positive correlation between common interests and success. Religion is one of the most important factors both in a person's background and in his present activities because it is concerned with basic attitudes and convictions."

Another marriage counselor tells us that he asked 750 couples what, in their opinion, was the greatest element for making happiness in family life. He reports that the largest number of those replying said, "Religion lived daily in the home." One of the most important things you will ever do is to plant your marriage firmly in spiritual soil where it may thrive. Religion is far more important in marriage than most people who are beginning their life together realize.

There are many reasons why your marriage should have a religious influence. Beyond a doubt, it is a very special step in life. Many things are tied to your marriage—your dreams, most meaningful desires, tenderest sentiments, highest values of your life, and, to a considerable extent, your future. If you would find roots for this most vital of all relationships, you must deal with the religious issues of life.

The more you understand these issues and the spiritual resources that come from a religiously oriented life, the more your marriage can be enriched with worthwhile things to assure domestic happiness. The presence of religious attitudes in the family life and fellowship based on these considerations encourage stability within its members. In study after study, church related families have been shown to be more stable than non-religiously-oriented families.

The Mixed-Marriage Problem

One of the most important elements in a marriage is the ability of each partner to enter enthusiastically into the life and interests of the other. When this is lacking, a vacuum is formed. This vacuum can be the beginning of serious problems and lead eventually to a marital breakup. In a religiously mixed marriage, complete compatibility is unlikely, in fact, almost impossible

Contemporary life has put people of various faiths side by side in everyday living. Such close association has led to the establishment of strong and enduring friendships among many young people. These friendships blossom into love. Young people become so emotionally involved they decide to go ahead and marry in spite of difficulties and complications concerning their religious life. Headaches and heartaches develop. Young people find themselves married and then are forced to open their eyes to the stern and stubborn realities of life which romantic love tends to ignore.

An interfaith marriage, like any marriage, occurs in the midst of a social environment. Other people are involved. There are two sets of parents who are interested in the new marriage and children who will be born to this marriage. Families visit one another. Grandchildren come. Some couples can make a successful adjustment in an interfaith marriage at first but find new difficulty when a child is born. The matter of the child's religious training and eventual church affiliation arises.

A few years ago a study was sponsored by an educational council among young people. The title of the study was "Youth Tell Their Story." The figures showed that where both sets of parents were either Catholic or Protestant (using this word in its broadest sense) approximately 6.6 percent of the parents were separated. In the case of mixed religions 15.2 percent of the marriages were broken. It should be remembered that these figures represented marriages with children. There seems no doubt that the figures would have been higher if the childless marriages had been included in the study. There are tremendous hazards involved and many adjustments to be made in any marriage, but the chances of the marriage's failure increase when it is a religiously mixed one. Surely, we should agree that if any set of complicating factors doubles or triples the prospects of failure, then a young couple, no matter how deeply in love, would do well to give serious consideration before exposing themselves to those factors.

An Even Worse Matter

The home's greatest religious problem today, however, is not that of mixed marriages. There is a new threat—far more dangerous to home life and especially to the well-being of children. It has been called by many names, but, in essence, it has one characteristic—a yielding to the spirit of the times. In earlier years we called it "worldliness." Today we are a bit more sophisticated in our terminology. Sometimes it is called "freedom from the shackles of institutionalism." Other times some call it "deliverance from the bondage of creeds," and a recent writer has called it "the liberation of man from religious and metaphysical tutelage, the turning of his attention away from other worlds and toward this one."

What is this so-called "new look" in religion? It is an attempt to rule out God completely—not by opposing him or arguing against his existence, but by simply regarding him as an unnecessary hypothesis entirely irrelevant to the need of modern man. The advanced sophisticates would not say "God is dead" but rather he has retired—to a statutory state of senility. A recent article in a contemporary periodical was entitled "Secularism—God Emeritus." This mood conveys the philosophy that the old God is harmless enough and may therefore be permitted to putter around a bit in what we formerly considered his laboratory, the world. These modern sophisticates would say that we do not expect anything very vital, startling, or important from him in the future. Thus, we shall not waste our energies in debate about the weight of his past contributions. We simply do not expect much meaningful activity from him in the forseeable future. We shall not oppose him, but we shall ignore him, as, it seems, we must. He is emeritus, retired, a spiritual has-been.

This new attitude is overflowing into the homelife of our nation. Parents are becoming unconcerned about their own spiritual life and indifferent to the spiritual training of their children. This guilt feeling of the parents because of their lingering sense of right and wrong causes them to become hostile. They begin to attack the church. Again, their approach is more sophisticated but basically it is the same old criticism.

The contemporary terminology of those who criticise the church is to speak of the "institutional church" as failing to meet the needs of modern man. When one hears this today, he is not quite sure what these self-styled critics mean. To be sure, churches have never done all that they should have done in any area of ministry. This, however, is because churches are made up of human beings—all fallible and incomplete. When our homes, however, are infiltrated with this subtle philosophy of being emancipated from the shackles of ecclesiasticism and religion, the home is in great danger. A marriage has a much greater chance to last and be happy if it has a healthy attitude toward religion and the churches.

Religion and Morals in Marriage

Although our country, according to many writers, is adopting a more permissive attitude toward sex, one fact is still true. A husband and wife expect sexual fidelity from each other. Even if one or both knows that the other has had sexual experience before marriage, extramarital relationships are not condoned by normally adjusted people today.

With due respect for all other causes leading to separation and divorce, adultery is still the one act that will destroy a marriage quicker than any other problem. It must, of course, be recognized that sometimes sexual infidelity is a symptom of other deep-seated shortcomings within the marriage relationship. Almost invariably, however, when these problems erupt into physical unfaithfulness, this act usually, if not always, takes over as the number one problem. Probably most counselors, if not all, follow the practice of this writer. One of the first questions in counseling those in marriage difficulty is, "Has there been physical unfaithfulness on the part of either or both members of the marriage?"

To say what religion in general teaches about sex is to enter into a long discussion. Some of the primitive religions were bound up very closely with the sex act. The temple girls, dedicated to their gods, were nothing more than religious prostitutes. The man worshiper actually engaged in sexual relations as a part of his act of worship. One thing is significant, however, about even these crude forms of religion. A man's wife was still his wife. There was no room within the religious framework for a woman to be unfaithful. Of course, the man was offered much more freedom.

It took Christianity, however, to bring full privileges to the woman. It seems safe to say that today all enlightened religions recognize that within the marriage framework there must be protection for both partners from a promiscuous companion. The very laws of morality and monogamy in our land are due to religious roots, especially Christianity. One shudders to think of the implication toward marriage laws that lie within the present movement to remove God from public life.

What keeps a man or woman moral? Is it fear of being caught and dragged into a divorce court? Certainly this is the only deterrent for some men—probably for some women also. Is it because a husband and wife are so much in love with each other they could not possibly dream of having an affair with someone else? In many cases this, no doubt, is true. It is probably more likely to be true with a woman than with most men. On the other hand, most marriages have had periods of tension and disagreement sufficient to tempt one or both companions to infidelity purely as an act of revenge if for no other reason.

What is the real reason married couples remain moral? There is only one fact that is sufficiently motivating to insure and assure complete fidelity. It is the conviction that God is holy and that we as mortal beings are subject to his sovereignty. As Christians, this sovereignty is reflected in the lordship of Jesus Christ. Remove this from one's life, and you have removed the strongest inducement to chastity and the greatest deterrent to immorality. If morality is the chief ally of the home, religion is the chief ally of morality, and, therefore, it is the one thing above all others a marriage must have if it is to be enduring.

Other Fruits of Faith

The matter of sexual morality is not, however, the only area in which marriage needs strength and discipline. Neither is it the only field to which religion makes a contribution. In *Building a Christian Home,* Martha Boone Leavell says, "With religion there is a new meaning to the thousand interests that occupy a family's life. The earth, the sky, the rocks, the arts; the history, science, language that come to be studied in the school; the progress, problems, the pleasures of the world of men all take on a new significance. . . . Religion will discard the bad and choose the best. Religion establishes taste for what is good."

What is the most important element in home life? Is it not the relationship between husband and wife? A couple genuinely dedicated to the principles of true religion can come nearer having harmony than anyone else. Relationships rooted in merely a psychological approach or even ethical content without the dynamic of religious experience will seldom be deep enough to weather the storm of domestic problems.

Great thinkers in all ages have recognized the need for religious motivation in life. Alexis Carrel says that it "brings to man an inner strength, spiritual life, ineffable peace." Thomas Fuller calls it "the best armor in the world" and Billy Graham says that there is "no common denominator in the world today except religion." Julius Charles calls man, without religion, "the creature of circumstances" and David Hume says, "Look for a people entirely destitute of religion, and if you find them at all, be assured they are but a few degrees removed from brutes." An aged Frenchman said, "I have lived long enough to know what I did not at one time believe—that no society can be upheld in happiness and honor without the sentiment of religion."

Is it training for our children the home seeks to give? It will take spiritual motivation to do the job well. The youth of our land cannot have a sound development of character or a fair American chance in life without religion. Educate children without religion and you make a race of clever devils out of them.

If we were to summarize in a few choice words that which the home needs in order to give it happiness in superlative form, could we do any better than call to mind the words Paul used in the book of Galatians—love, joy, peace, patience, kindness, generosity, faithfulness, tolerance or gentleness, and self-control. All of these come not from mere human wisdom but from the presence of divine strength in the life enabling these virtues to be achieved.

Your Home and Jesus

Thus far in this book the writer has refrained from preaching. This has been difficult since he is a pastor and for many years has delivered three sermons every Sunday. Also, in this last chapter the writer has mainly sought to discuss religion in general rather than Christianity in particular. These last words, however, will be not a sermon but a testimony concerning his Christian faith.

Any religious philosophy which is rooted and grounded in morality and ethics should certainly help bring stability and endurance to the home. Any concept of God which recognized his holiness should influence the domestic situation for good and permanence. The highest revelation of God, however, is found in Jesus Christ. As a Christian, one cannot compromise on this cardinal fact.

With all due respect for every other cause in this world that is working for good, it is the religion of Jesus Christ lived conscientiously that will most help the family cope with conflicts, face domestic problems, and develop attitudes which bring harmony in family life. Many problems in the home could have been avoided if a genuine Christian approach had been taken by each member. It is more than a pious truism to say that our world's greatest need is for Christian homes.

What does it mean to have a Christian home? Let it be underscored that having a Christian home means far more than a houseful of nice people who treat each other fairly kindly and who go to church fairly regularly. It means a home where Christ is known, loved and served. It is a place where children come to know him through their parents and where Christian training of the children is placed ahead of the social ambition of the father. In a Christian home, the father is determined to carry on his business in conformity with the mind of Christ and where both father and mother are determined to make their social life conform to high Christian ideals. In a Christian home, far horizons of a world are to be won for Christ.

The real problem in having a Christian home is to get people to take seriously their Christian faith and live in a way that is consistent with their profession and worship. It is not that Christianity has tried and has failed. It is rather that Christianity has been found difficult and in too many cases has not been tried. Have you ever heard of the soap maker who ran out of superlatives to define his product? He created a statement that said in a new way the final word that could be stated about it. He said, "Since we could not improve our product, we improved the box." We can never improve the message of Christ and the content of our faith. We can, however, improve the container. We can yield ourselves to the control and power and lordship of the living Christ in family relationships. It is the "box" that is seen. Thus, the box is that which must be made attractive. Our homes can be a bit of heaven here on earth when we live in such a way that people lose sight of us and "see the Christ instead."

You want your marriage to be always at its best. Actually, this most meaningful of all relationships has the most extreme of potentialities—it may be the best or the worst of all experiences known to man. If a marriage is marked by love, mutual trust, sympathy, understanding, gentleness, and forbearance, the relationship bears a similarity to Christ and his bride. On the other hand, if there is bickering and contention, fussing and fighting, suspicion and misunderstanding, there is untold misery. The ideal Christian marriage is when a man loves his wife as Christ loved the church. There has never been a love so pure, clean, holy, and happy as that of the Savior for those for whom he died. The husband is commanded in the New Testament to love his wife as Christ loved the church, and the wife is commanded to be faithful unto the husband even as the church is obedient unto Christ in all things.

If Jesus is the Lord of life in your home, your marriage can be beautiful. For such a home to break up is unthinkable. Marriages do not fail. People fail. The institution of marriage will continue regardless of the cynical attitude that some take toward it. Even in the midst of our sexual revolution and the proclamation of a "new morality," there are and will continue to be many couples who take Christ seriously in their marriage relationship and will have marriages that last and homes that are joyful. Will you be one of these?

About the Author

GROWING A LIFE TOGETHER is a natural outgrowth of Fred M. Wood's counseling and pastoral background. Here he provides practical help for newlyweds or those planning to marry, carrying the reader through courtship into marriage and into the future.

Dr. Fred M. Wood, a native of Memphis, has served since 1952 as pastor of the Eudora Baptist Church, Memphis, Tennessee. He is a graduate of Union University and Southern Baptist Theological Seminary, institutions where he received B.A., B.D., Th.M., and Th.D. degrees. Union University bestowed the D.D. on Dr. Wood in 1952. Before going to Eudora, he was pastor at Dresden, Tennessee.

He has served as president of the Tennessee Baptist Convention, and has had many positions in denominational and interdenominational life.

He is married to the former Lillie Belle Johnson. The Woods have two sons, Fred Mitchell Wood, Jr., and David Johnson Wood.

GROWING A LIFE TOGETHER is Dr. Wood's sixth book for Broadman. *The Glory of Galatians* and *Dynamic Living for Difficult Days* are available in addition to this book. He is also a contributor to *The Teacher's Bible Commentary.*